Unconditional Dad

A Father and Pastor's Journey
Through the Words: "Dad, I'm Gay"

Chris Rader

To

Clarence L. Rader

Thank you for showing me

what it means to be an

Unconditional Dad.

Contents

Average Day

S *unday, November 22, 2009, 6 A.M.* Somewhere between sleep and consciousness, I notice my wife is already awake and looking at me with her gentle eyes as if to say, *I still* love you. Typically, I'm the one who's up before the alarm, and she's the one who doesn't move until the smell of coffee reaches the upstairs. It's still mostly dark outside with scattered sunshine in the forecast, and the tip of my nose is telling me it's cold out there—at least by San Diego standards. Before I can engage my brain into analyzing why this day is off to an unusual start, I begin to hibernate back under the covers and disengage. Decision made: I am sleeping in today!

But a gentle touch and a soft voice encourages me otherwise, "We need to be at church in less than an hour."

I don't want to go! "But you have to." *No I don't.* "Are you sick?" *Yeah...really sick, I'm staying home today.* "But you can't do that. You're the pastor." *Oh yeah. (heavy sigh.)*

Fortunately, I'm the children's pastor, so there's a lot of grace in a room full of third, fourth, and fifth graders. As long as my story illustration includes a sugared food product, I'll still be a hero!

After two high-energy services and a long lunch meeting with several of our key ministry volunteers, I head home. As an extreme introvert who's already spent most of his *limited* extroverted energy, I need to power down and recharge my batteries. *I feel a nap coming on!*

Exhausted, I arrive home and am greeted by my faithful dog, Sherman, who loves me in spite of my crankiness. My wife (who volunteers with the two year olds at our church) greets me in the kitchen, and we exchange stories about some of the funny things the kids said or did this morning. After a pause in the conversation, I see that look on her face again. It's the same look I saw this morning, only now it's saying, *I still love you...and... we need to talk.*

My mind races through the list of "biggies." Divorce? *No.* Car accident? *No.* Cancer? *Maybe...but I doubt it.* When my list is exhausted, I feel the presence of God touch my shoulder as if to say, "You might want to sit down."

Somewhere between standing and sitting, I remember a conversation I had with God 17 years ago—shortly after our older son's birth. At that time, I was in the middle of writing an ethics paper on homosexuality for my master's program, and my wife brought Seth to me for some father-son bonding time. This conversation with God was more of a communication without any instructions about what to do, leaving me in an open cadence—a feeling of unresolvedness. My mind shifts back to my wife.

On this day my wife says, "It's our son." I know without a doubt that she means Seth (translated "appointed one" in Hebrew). As I make contact with the chair, I know the words that are now forming in my wife's mind and about to be spoken:

"He's gay."

As I sit for what seems like an eternity, my wife explains how she'd been helping Seth with his college applications a few days earlier. She noticed that he'd checked the boxes next to the names of some social groups, indicating that he'd be interested in receiving more information.

Photography. *No surprise there.*

Christian fellowships. *Good.*

GLBT. *Surprise!*

As my wife recounts her conversation with Seth, her eyes well up as she confesses to not handling it very well. She knew I had a busy weekend, so she'd decided it was best to wait until after church today to discuss this issue with me.

Who can find a virtuous wife?

For her worth *is* far above rubies.

The heart of her husband safely trusts her.

Proverbs 31:10-11

Seth has kept this issue from us for two years. For him, that was the safest route. His mother has known for three whole days—and the anticipation has been building. Now Sunday afternoon has finally arrived. So after what seems like half an eternity, my conversation with my wife ends, and I begin the long walk up the stairs toward my son's room.

I have a momentary flashback.

As a child I once got in trouble for something, and my mom uttered the dreaded words: "Wait until your father comes home!" Upon hearing Dad's car turn into the driveway at the end of the day, I ran upstairs to my room. Indiscernible voices seeped through the floorboards, followed by the approaching sound of heavy footsteps. Almost 50 years later, I still remember the anticipation, fear, and anxiety. Strange that I cannot remember what happened after my dad opened the door...

I wonder:

What's going through Seth's mind? Is he afraid? I thought we had a good father-son relationship. Have I ever given him the impression that he can't come to me with anything and everything? Seems as though most, if not all, teenagers reach a point in life when they decide they can't tell Dad something. But during our "guy times" I thought I'd done a good job of communicating the "You can come to me with anything" promise...

Navigating the stairs seems unusually difficult. I pause after reaching the landing and take a deep breath. As I turn to the right and step toward his room, I think of my training and research on the issue of homosexuality. Everything I've been taught indicates environmental factors. For instance, an absent or abusive father may cause a person's "decision" to enter the gay lifestyle.

All of my training and research just got tossed in the trash.

As I open the bedroom door and enter his room, I tell Seth that his mother and I just finished talking. He nods indicating that he already knew this. And then our conversation consumes the other half of eternity. So many questions, so few words. A lot of heavy silence. Most of what we discuss enters my heart, but unfortunately it isn't recorded in my brain for further review.

Here's what I do remember:

"Dad, it wasn't you."

Why didn't you come and tell me?

"Dad, I *know* what you believe."

All I've ever wanted to be was a father who let his kids know that he loves them unconditionally—and in the moment when my son needed his father most, all he saw was…a judgmental pastor.

The Words

Every day I play the scene over and over again in my head. Even though most of it is foggy, there's a sense that something is left unresolved. It wasn't until I wrote down the title of this book that I realized that Seth has (still) never actually uttered those words, "Dad, I'm gay."

Maybe it's because we're both conflict-avoiders and are content to look around the elephant in the room. Maybe the opportunity just hasn't come up. Then again, maybe fear or something else has entombed these words under lock and key.

I tried to speak words of unconditional love, but I don't think that's what Seth heard.

As I look back over the events of 2010, I realize that God is deeply interested in how I respond to my son as a father.

I believe God is equally interested in how I—as a Christian and a pastor—am doing as His ambassador in relation to the gay and lesbian community. *There is a lot of room for improvement.* Still, after an intense season of wrestling with God, I have few answers and more questions.

While I may not have sought this path, it appears to have chosen me. The following chapters reveal my Journey through these three words that I still haven't heard my son speak—and yet somehow they drive me to seek God on a deeper level every day. I have reached a place of peace, living within the mystery of God. *Mystery of God* doesn't mean the absence of meaning or understanding; instead, it's the presence of more meaning than I can comprehend.[1]

In the weeks, months, and years to come, I choose to seek more of the presence of God and trust that the meaning will come when God chooses to reveal it. Meanwhile...

My name is Chris Rader and this is *my* Journey.

The Starting Point

So how does one start a book about a topic that's dividing our country, our culture, and now my home? First, by stating that it's not intended to persuade, support, refute, or change anybody's position on human sexuality as it relates to God or the Bible.

This is *my* story.

YouTube videos show picketers carrying signs that say JESUS HATES FAGS while protesting at a parade where men wear G-strings and pole dance on a float. Neither group accurately reflects the larger communities they purpose to represent, which makes it easy for us to marginalize them. That is, until one of the groups is viewed through the lens of *this is my son.*

As a dad, how do I show unconditional love to my son? Definitional boundaries of terms such as *unconditional* are constantly being rebuilt and expanded. Suddenly, I find myself in the crossfire of rhetoric between the church and the GLBT (Gay, Lesbian, Bisexual and Transgender) community. Hurtful speech is lobbed back and forth like grenades, which leaves me feeling caught in the middle and helpless.

As a pastor, how do I resolve this dissonant chord between the church and the GLBT community? I don't want this! Yet I cannot ignore it. I will not turn my back on my son. I cannot abandon my God. This I do know:

1. There is a God.
2. He hears my pain.
3. He loves my son.
4. This will work out for a purpose that is far beyond my pain, far beyond my son's sexuality, and part of a much bigger plan that I obviously don't understand yet.

But for now I feel alone, abandoned by God, cast adrift by the church, and, as a pastor, despised by the GLBT community. I tell my son I love him "unconditionally." Somehow in the communication it must sound to him more like, "I love you unconditionally...*except* for this."

I desire to create some space in my life for God to do that which only God can do. God, I trust You with my life to do with as You please. I trust You with my son. Not knowing the depths or heights to which this Journey will take me—*Sua Sponte!*[2]

I Am My Father's Son

The summer of 1965 was coming to an end. My excitement had been building all year: I'd be starting kindergarten next month! No more being the only kid in the neighborhood who had to stay home and play alone in the backyard. While I was glad that summer was rapidly unwinding, I wanted this particular night to last forever.

It was getting dark, and we needed to get home. Dad and I were on our way home from *our adventure*. I don't remember the exact mission; it was top secret. Not even my older brother or sisters were allowed to know the exact details. We were only a few blocks from home when Dad unexpectedly pulled the car to the side of the road. He told me to grab the secret package out of the backseat. We'd be walking from here.

This is great! I never get alone time with Dad. He's always working, and when he isn't working, my brother gets to go with him and I have to stay home. Mom says I'm too little to go. "Am not!" So now we're going stealth! No lights and no noise of the engine to give us away.

We began making our way to safety under the cover of darkness. We played Kick the Can and I Spy for what seemed like forever. We talked about the challenges of kindergarten. My brother and sisters had already informed me about what to expect and told me I should be glad that I'll have Mrs. Dorman (apparently the better of the two kindergarten teachers). After hearing my dad's stories about attending school in a one-room schoolhouse (and walking to school in the snow...uphill...both ways), I felt the need to bring my dad up to speed. Things aren't the way they used to be, Dad! After all, this *is* the '60s.

When I grow up, I'm going to have a son, and we're going to go on our own missions just like this. I love you, Dad.

I Am My Son's Father

January 14, 2004. "Your mission…should you choose to accept it…!" *Just you and me, son.*

Before Seth and I left on our mission, I felt the need to call my dad. I remembered how he once carved out a special time just for me, and now I was going to do that with my son.

Our phone conversation about our mission 39 years earlier did not go as I'd expected. Dad had a totally different take on it. Apparently, Mom had sent us to pick up something from the store. But on the way home, the car ran out of gas. So Dad let it drift to the side of the road, we locked the doors, and the car sat there until payday. And while I was kicking a can, Dad was apparently thinking about how he was going to get to work the next day.

Now Seth and I were off on our own adventure. Driving east, we arrived at Pine Valley Camp just before sunset. There were remnants indicating that a weekend youth retreat had just ended. The air was crisp and quiet. Our cabin was simple: one bed, two bunk beds. A rustic desert picture was nailed to the wall. A room heater pinged and banged when it kicked on, but at least it worked. We threw our sleeping bags in the corner and unloaded our stash of snack food onto the bed.

Soon my son would be a teenager. So that night and the next day we'd talk about what it means to be a godly man. I even brought along a tape series to lead our discussions. We'd talk about character issues such as respect, honor, and integrity; the difference between courting and dating; and the institution of marriage. We'd cover more difficult topics, too, such as masturbation and homosexuality. But in between our discussions, we played ping-pong and foosball and rode the tire swing. We ate junk food, went out for pizza at midnight, and stayed up as late as we wanted. In the end it was mission accomplished! *I love you, son.*

Sex. Drugs. Rock-'n'-roll. Every generation has its issues. Throughout our weekend together, I found myself wondering, *How do I protect my son? How do I equip him to handle what life will throw at him? He's so innocent, yet growing up so fast. How will he respond when a good friend offers him alcohol? Drugs? What about peer pressure? Rejection? Those are only some of the issues I had to deal with at his age. Now teens have to navigate the Internet and social media as well.* Suddenly feeling ill-equipped for the job of "Dad," I think, *How much of this weekend will he even remember?*

Yet, when we drove back home, I wanted Seth to know two things: First, I love him unconditionally. Nothing he can ever do or say will change that fact. And second, whatever the topic, no matter how uncomfortable or difficult it may be, he can always talk to me about anything.

Men...De

November 22, 2009. Leaving Seth's room, having just confirmed the unimaginable, I close my bedroom door and collapse on the bed. Every fiber of my body writhes in pain. I jam my face into the pillow, trying to muffle the sounds of my sobbing. I force my face deeper into the pillow until I cannot breathe. Pausing, I gasp for air. I scream again before the first sounds have echoed back. Thousands of voices are talking in my head, each one trying to be heard over the others. Rapid-fire questions. Statements. Pieces of information.

Crying. Screaming. I've lost control of my breathing. What was second nature has now become a battle I must win—and quickly. *Focus! Breathe! Sob! Scream!* I'm stuck in that space between getting enough air and passing out. It's a moment that spans the universe. I'd settle for either, yet I'm suspended in a moment of purgatory. It goes on. And on. And on. *Can someone save me from myself? Shake me out of my emotional trance? I need a kick to bring me out of my dream. Does anyone hear my pain? Does anyone care?*

In the breaths between screams, the voices become clearer. The words and sentences are still scrambled together, yet there seems to be two distinct voices. One voice (*men*, or more literally translated "on the one hand...") is random. *Not good. Unconnected words. Incomplete sentences. Dangling participles. Thought pictures without words.* The other voice (*de*, or more literally translated "on the other hand...") is steady, almost a hushed, syncopated monotone.[3] Good. It's not competing for space. A lighthouse. A calming, rhythmic familiarity. *Focus on the light!*

Men: How could this happen?

De: Before I formed your son in the womb, I knew him.[4]

Men: I did everything right! I read all of the parenting books and listened to the tapes on raising boys.

De: No one does *everything* right.[5]

Men: I wasn't abusive. I wasn't absent. I love my son!

De: I know. I love My Son, too.[6]

Men: This can't possibly end well for my son. Will he die of
AIDS?

De: Everyone dies. This isn't the end.[7]

Men: I know he didn't choose this. If he *was* born with this,
does that make it okay? Natural? Is this similar to being
born left-handed or being born with cancer? Aren't there
studies that show a genetic propensity toward alcohol?
Either way, does that make it right?

De: He didn't choose this; I chose him.[8]

Men: How long has my son known? When did he start having
these thoughts? Why didn't he come to me and tell me?
Has he acted on it yet?

De: Too many questions. Run-on sentences.[9]

Men: Can people change their sexuality? *Should* they? Does
it matter?

De: All will be changed anyway.[10]

Men: Have You turned Your back on my son?

De: I will never leave him; I have never abandoned him.[11]

Men: I don't understand!

De: My ways are beyond what you can comprehend.[12] I
know you don't see it, but I *am* working this out for *My*
purpose, not yours.[13]

Men: Why would You do this to my son? Do You love my
    son?

De: One answer leads to a thousand questions. I'm just going
    to wrap My arms around you as a mother does to a two
    year old in the midst of a temper tantrum. When you're
    done flailing your arms and legs and have exhausted all
    of your tears, when your screams die down and your
    body goes limp, then we'll continue this conversation.

Men: I have nothing left. I cannot carry this burden.

De: I never intended for you to carry this burden alone. Give
    your burden to Me. I will give you rest along the way.[14]

I feel as though I've just collapsed on the beach after a
(verbal) near drowning. My body sinks into the sand, unable
to move. Body, mind, and soul are emptied. His gentle yet
firm hands do the heavy lifting, taking what is left of me to
a place of rest.

I push the pillow aside and take a deep, gentle breath.
Somehow we'll get through this. Thus ends the third cry.

Defining Moments

In March 2009, DreamWorks Animation released the movie *Monsters vs Aliens*. Early in the film, the heroine, Susan, is about to marry Derek. As she steps outside the church for a moment, a meteor hits her—literally. But she brushes herself off and finishes getting ready for her big day. Then as she's standing at the altar and getting ready to say, "I do," Derek says, "Susan, you're...you're glowing....No, I mean you're really glowing! You're green!" Suddenly Susan grows to gigantic proportions, breaks through the roof of the church, and keeps going until she's nearly 10 stories tall. Her happily ever after has been delayed. Indefinitely. Now her self-centered fiancée wants nothing to do with her, and he abandons her in her time of need. The meteor has altered the coordinates of Susan's life. The door to the past is forever closed. Happily ever after is gone. The future is at best unknown.

But life isn't over for Susan. Within the movie's 95 minutes running time, she not only saves the world and makes some unusual friends, but also learns a great deal about herself. Susan finds an inner confidence that Derek's dreams and career goals had previously overshadowed. Near the end of the movie, Susan accepts her new way of life as a giant. And when given the opportunity to go back to "normal," she declines. *(Sorry! Seven years spent working as a children's pastor means that most of my analogies come from animated movies!)*

> We were designed to live through something,
>
> and the thing we were meant to live through
>
> was designed to change us.[15]
>
> —Donald Miller, *A Million Miles in*
> *a Thousand Years*

People get hit by metaphoric "meteors" all the time. I've never been one who believes in luck, good or bad. I believe everything and everyone is created with intent and has a purpose and meaning.[16] That's all well and good until something happens that appears random, unexpected, or uninvited.

When we get a *lucky* break, we're excited. New possibilities are available to us. Doors of opportunity have been opened. Our course of life has been altered for the good. Or so we think. Yet when *bad luck* appears, we get discouraged. This is *not* what we wanted. Luck (either good or bad) alters our destination. It moves us into a place where we did not boldly choose to go.

It's not so much that situations can be defined as being good or bad "luck," but rather as intentional instead of random. We label things "bad" when they're inconvenient and unscheduled destinations on *our* road maps of life. We're not aware of a bigger purpose, and we get frustrated when our life maps go in a different direction than what we believed was God's plan. Events are designed to move us into a place where we may not wish to go. Yet God's purpose and intention is for us to navigate the good *and* the bad, the intentional and the "random" in order to accomplish His purposes, not ours.[17]

The story of Job is a classic example of "bad luck." Job was a wealthy man. One day his sons and daughters were having a party at the oldest brother's house when life began to unravel. Before the sun set that day, a series of tragic events had unfolded. Bandits stole all of Job's cattle and killed his fieldworkers. A "chance" lightning storm started a fire that killed all of his sheep and the people attending them. More bandits took Job's camels. A rogue wind knocked down the roof of Job's oldest son's house killing all of Job's sons and daughters inside. That sure sounds like a string of bad luck to me! How else can you explain what happened?

But before all of this occurs, we read that God and Satan had a discussion about Job. God asked: "Have you considered My servant Job?" (Job 1:8) Basically, God bragged to Satan about Job being a faithful believer and servant of God. Satan responded by saying Job only serves God because God has given him good luck. Job wouldn't be so faithful if *bad* luck happened to him! So God grants Satan permission to bring bad luck on Job with the intention of proving Satan wrong.

After all that Satan threw at him, Job's wife gave him this advice: "Do you still hold fast to your integrity? Curse God and die!" (Job 2:9) *Thanks for the encouragement… I love you, too!* Then Job's friends came by to cheer him up. They told him that everything that happened was most likely a result of something wrong in Job's life. Perhaps these calamities were a result of Job's bad choices, a bad environment, Job's sin, bad karma, and so on. *Thanks, guys. Appreciate ya! I'm hurting here, and I could sure use a little kindness instead of judgment from my "friends."*[18]

So Job spent some time in introspection and spiritual evaluation, and he came to the conclusion that as best as he could tell, he hadn't done anything wrong.

When you're hit by the meteors of life,

your response unfolds your core values

and your true beliefs about God's character.[19]

As I write this chapter, there's a story in the news about a young man who committed suicide. He took the ultimate "out." He was a superstar on his high school and college football teams, and he'd been doing well in the NFL, too. But he was hampered with injuries. This guy had his whole life ahead of him when the meteor of adversity (injuries) hit. What he did next revealed his core beliefs about God.

When the meteors of life (large or small) hit, am I willing to adjust? Am I willing to alter the course of my life in order to align it with where God is moving and what He is doing? Will I get beyond just recognizing that God is trying to get my attention and be obedient to move in that direction? Or will I consider the ultimate "out"?

Meteors, those Defining Moments, aren't always convenient. In fact, they usually strike at very inconvenient times. Sometimes Defining Moments hit you, and sometimes (this is where the meteor analogy breaks down) you have to grab hold of them as they present themselves—as if they were portkeys.

In *Harry Potter and the Goblet of Fire*, Harry and Cedric Diggory grab hold of a portkey thinking it's the prize to the Triwizard Tournament. They expect to be teleported to the Winner's Circle, but instead, it teleports them to a cemetery where Harry is confronted by his enemy—"He-Who-Must-Not-Be-Named." Harry reached out to seize an opportunity, only it didn't play out the way he expected. Nonetheless, it was a Defining Moment that strengthened Harry to meet future foes. Harry was meant to live through it. It was designed (by the writer) to change Harry. It was necessary to strengthen Harry for what lies ahead. *(It's not an animated movie. But it's still a children's ministry analogy.)*

So as I was proofing this manuscript early one morning, I was contemplating the whole idea of Defining Moments and meteor strikes in my life. I created a list of them, a sort of spiritual inventory. (I'll explain these later in the book). Many were large meteors; I had little or no control over them. Others were not so large and required only minor adjustments to my life. And some were more like portkeys, which I needed to grab onto. What follows is a description of one such portkey.

One morning I had an 11:30 meeting with the other pastors and leaders at my church (Journey Community Church in La Mesa, California). It's a routine meeting that's scheduled every Wednesday—nothing out of the ordinary. But on this particular day, we were going to be discussing (at least in part) my transition from Children's Ministry to more of a Pastoral Care Ministry (PCM) role. This would include helping people navigate tragedy, addiction, loss, grief, and so on. We were planning to go over a timeline of the events that we'd discussed earlier in the week and figure out when we might begin this new ministry.

But as I started my day, my heart was unsettled. As I prayed, I sensed that I needed some dialogue time with God.

I needed to adjust my morning and carve out some time just to listen.

I listen best when I get my focus off of myself and my to-do list. And the best way I've found to do that is by climbing Cowles Mountain. It's close to my house, and it requires hiking approximately a mile and a half of switchbacks to get to the top. About halfway up, I'm able to focus specifically on my breathing, and most of the noise of the day has been removed. Then I spend time at the top praying and seeking God's direction.

Here is my account for the events that unfolded on that particular morning:

Journal Entry—January 5, 2011
Today started with a brisk hike up Cowles Mtn. My best time in months—28 mins. I have some regularly scheduled mtgs today, nothing out of the ordinary. But my prayer up the mtn today was "God...I want to know what You want me to do *today*. I am available. I have no agenda. I have things I 'want' to do, things I think I 'need' to do, but ultimately I want to be available to You."...I'm sensing God has a different plan for me today.

I went home, showered, and headed out to work. I traveled north from my house and crossed over a major intersection, and there was a truck stopped/ parked in the left lane, a couple of people were crossing the street in a hurried manner...something wasn't right. I looked past the truck, and there was a body in the street—from what I could tell, an elderly female. She was unconscious, and her arms and legs weren't in normal positions. I assumed the truck hit her. Defining Moment! I could make a right turn and keep on going, get on with my day (parable of the Good Samaritan went through my head)...I justified my thoughts as I probably should get out of the way as paramedics and police cars would be showing up any second. "I'll pray for them!" *Typical pastor response.* OR...I could adjust my day and grab onto the portkey. I decided to grab on.

"Don" was the driver of the truck. He's in his 60s; a big guy. His assumption was he'd just killed this woman. From the looks of her, I would have come to the same conclusion. He was crying, screaming, and becoming a little disoriented, heading toward trauma/shock. I saw a woman calling 911. Another woman tried to get a blanket on the lady and figure out how to administer CPR without causing more damage. Perhaps CPR wasn't even necessary. I went over to Don to try and get him under control. Traffic was starting to back up. I went back to the street and diverted traffic into a neighborhood and away from the scene. A man came out of the parking lot across the way and offered to take over with the traffic if I'd go over and take care of Don who was increasingly losing control.

Don was asking the "why" questions. He was also punching his truck, hitting his head on the front fender, falling to the ground, and then punching the ground. Don handed me his driver's license and directed me to find his insurance information in the glove box. That's when I found out his name is Don. I told him that I'm a pastor and I'm here to help. He asked me if I'm a "real" Christian...a born-again kind, not some new-ager. He asked if Jesus is my "Lord." I said "Yes." He (bear) hugged me for what seemed like hours. I began to cry with him, and I felt in a sense that I was helping relieve some of the steam from the kettle. "Weep with those who weep." Eventually the scene was swarming with officers and paramedics. Don was still banging his head and hands on the truck and seemingly out of control. The officers told Don he needed to pull it together or they'd have to handcuff him and put him in the vehicle so he wouldn't hurt anyone, including himself. My job became clear: Keep Don from being handcuffed and keep him engaged in conversation. The ambulance drove away with its lights and sirens going. I took that as a good sign. If they're in a hurry, there was a chance she was still alive. Without a miracle, I didn't see her surviving.

Everyone was catching their breath and calming down. I met with the detective, and she took my testimony. I assured Don that if he needed lunch or a ride home, I'd be glad to provide that. Then I walked to my car and got on with my day.

Don kept asking the "why" question. I doubt we'll know the full answer to that question for a long time, if ever. But I encouraged him to keep looking for God's fingerprint in the midst of the chaos. Don had "lost it." He needed someone at that moment. I was able to comfort and assure him that God sees his pain and sent me to be there for him.

I arrived at work, and my meeting was already in progress. I'm not sure what I missed, and at that point I didn't care. My heart was still racing. *So this is what my new role as "care" pastor is going to look like?* I think my start date for this new ministry began this morning! *This is draining.*

Later that day, I received an e-mail from Don. The following are some excerpts from his email and my response.

Dear Chris,

Thank God for your presence today. You helped me get through the worst trauma of my life. The officer at the scene later confirmed that the woman I hit had died....I am one of those selfish, half-hearted Christians...and this was a wake-up call. I had fooled myself into believing that God and I were on good terms. I know you will pray for me and for this person's loved ones. God bless you for that.

Don

Don,

I don't think it was by "chance" that we met. We may not have all the answers as to "why" just yet, and perhaps we won't know all of it this side of heaven. But in situations like this, I look for God's hand in it—in the midst of the chaos, pain, and tragedy, where do I see God? Not that God has to "fix" this or "remove" this, but God—just let me know that You are in the midst of it because I can't get through this without Your help.

Don, this is what I call a Defining Moment. Some would call it a Crisis of Belief. Something happens in life that shakes us to our very foundation to examine our core beliefs. It's when God reaches into your life to get your attention, in a manner you'd rather He not do. While this moment was tragic, I think God is interested in how you respond. What you do next defines what you really believe about God. In the Bible, Job experienced a tragedy beyond imagination. Job's wife responded, "Curse God and die," while Job responded, "How can I accept good from God without the adversity?" (Job 2:9-10) If you don't believe in a loving God who desires a close relationship with you, who cares about you, then you will look at this only as a tragedy. But God has a way of turning tragedy around to accomplish His purpose. If I believe that God loves me and has my eternal best interests at heart, then I will see His hand in the midst of it. God knew this would shake you to the core and that you would need someone there to help walk you through it. And God rearranged my day to make that happen.

Earlier that day I was praying: *Lord, I have some meetings today, nothing out of the "routine." I sense you have something different for me today. Help me to not only see it, but walk in it.* When I pulled up behind your truck and saw the woman in the street, I knew right away why God had me there.

"We were designed to live through something, and the things we live through were designed to change us." (Donald Miller)

There is no <edit> or <undo> in this life. There is no going back to "normal." There is only going forward.

You were designed by God to live through this. God is in the midst of doing something, and this was His wake-up call or invitation for you to join Him. As you process the accident, as you grieve the loss of life, look for God's hand in the midst of it. He IS there. The God I know has not abandoned you in the midst of this. In fact, He is seeking you out. God will not leave you nor forsake you in the coming days, weeks, or months. Seek Him and He will be found!

It's OK to grieve. It's OK to be angry with God (i.e., How did this happen? Why me?). At least you recognize there is a God who is in control even if/when you don't understand it. Talk with your pastor. I am more than available if you need or want to talk.

Our leadership team has and will be praying for you, Don.

Talk with you soon.
Chris

The Weaver

My life is just a weaving
Between my Lord and me.
I cannot change the colour
For He works most steadily.

Oft times He weaves the sorrow
And I in foolish pride
Forget He sees the upper
And I the underside.

Until the loom is silent
And the shuttle cease to fly,
Will God roll back the canvas
And explain the reason why.

The dark threads are as needful
In the skillful Weaver's Hand
As the golden threads of silver
He has patterned in His Plan.[20]

Sometimes we ask ourselves, *How come God isn't doing anything in my life? Why don't I sense God's presence in my life as so-and-so does?* The problem is not that God isn't working or that God isn't interested in us. The issue is more that we are just too busy or too unwilling to alter our schedule to allow God to interrupt our day. God asks us to "grab on." Then we check our Day-Timer or our PDA, and we just don't have time. We try to schedule an appointment for God the following week, but God's work continues all around us. And He invites us into His work.

Sometimes we need to grab the portkey. Other times God has to hit us with a meteor. Either way, one of our first Defining Moments has to answer the question, *Who is in charge of my life?* If I'm in the driver's seat, then I will see only tragedy in this kind of situation. I will be too busy with my agenda to see God's hand in the midst of what seems like chaos.

As a young child, having grown up as a churchgoer, I knew all the stories about Jesus. I believed that Jesus was part of the Creator who stepped out of eternity and into His creation. He didn't just tell us there is a better way. He didn't just dictate a book of instructions for us to follow. He showed us the way to go. Jesus said, "I *am* the way."[21]

I believed that Jesus died on the cross to make restitution for my mistakes, shortcomings, and yes, sins. But there is a difference between knowing it as information and acting on it as a core belief. If you confess with your mouth Jesus as *Lord* and you believe in your heart that God raised Him from the dead, then you will be saved.[22] Believing is not enough. Confessing Jesus as Lord means He drives, and I ride along. Giving up the steering wheel is not something that comes naturally to us. Sometimes we have to get hit by a meteor.

The Road of Life

At first, I saw God as my observer, my judge, keeping track of the things I did wrong, so as to know whether I merited heaven or hell when I die. He was out there sort of like a president. I recognized His picture when I saw it, but I really didn't know Him.

But later on when I met Christ, it seemed as though life were rather like a bike ride, but it was a tandem bike, and I noticed that Christ was in the back helping me pedal.

I don't know just when it was that He suggested we change places, but life has not been the same since.

When I had control, I knew the way. It was rather boring, but predictable. It was the shortest distance between two points.

But when He took the lead, He knew delightful long cuts, up mountains, and through rocky places at breakneck speeds, it was all I could do to hang on! Even though it looked like madness, He said, "Pedal!"

I worried and was anxious and asked, "Where are you taking me?" He laughed and didn't answer, and I started to learn to trust.

I forgot my boring life and entered into the adventure. And when I'd say, "I'm scared," He'd lean back and touch my hand.

He took me to people with gifts that I needed, gifts of healing, acceptance, and joy. They gave me gifts to take on my journey, my Lord's and mine.

And we were off again. He said, "Give the gifts away; they're extra baggage, too much weight." So I did, to the people we met and I found that in giving I received, and still our burden was light.

I did not trust Him, at first, to control my life. I thought He'd wreck it; but He knows bike secrets, knows how to make it bend to take sharp corners, knows how to jump to clear high rocks, knows how to fly to shorten scary passages.

And I am learning to shut up and pedal to the strangest places. And I'm beginning to enjoy the view and the cool breeze on my face with my delightful constant companion, Jesus Christ.

And when I'm sure I just can't do anymore, He just smiles and says…"Pedal!"

—Author Unknown[23]

Between Lands

E very summer our church is a host site for the Global Leadership Summit.[24] The Summit is a multi-day event during which pastors, diplomats, corporate executives, and directors of nonprofit or nongovernmental organizations talk about what it means to lead in their corner of the world. The goal is to help those who are in positions of leadership or influence lead with all diligence.[25]

In August 2010, I sat in a room with 300 other people, from all over Southern California, who wanted to learn how to be better leaders personally, corporately, and spiritually. The opening session, hosted by Bill Hybels, was intimidating, engaging, and thought provoking. Then a couple more sessions went by and the day progressed smoothly — as it had during the last seven years I'd attended this conference. However, I was now feeling a little nervous because every year there'd been one speaker, one drama, or one song that caused me to "train wreck." In other words, my wheels come off the track, and I have to change the way I do my life.

During a break between sessions, the band started playing a song to encourage everyone to take their seats. It was "Hosanna" by Hillsong. *Not again.* We sing this song at our church, and I'd made the "mistake" one day of turning the lyrics into a prayer. *I'm not going to be able to get through this!* I was standing among friends, singing along. Then somewhere in the middle, the lyrics "break my heart for what breaks Yours..." crushed me. My knees buckled, and I had to sit down. Leaning my head on the back of the chair in front of me, I hid my tears.

Get it together, Chris. This is a "leadership" summit. I don't think blubbering is going to raise your leadership stock. What is the person next to me thinking? Why is that song...those lyrics...so debilitating every time I hear it?

I pulled myself together as the next speaker was introduced: Jeff Manion. He'd be speaking from his book *The Land Between: Finding God in Difficult Transitions.* Jeff then described in great detail my current season of life. Suddenly it was as if the room was empty and Jeff was talking only to me. I hung on to every word. *How does he know?* He described the Land Between as a place "where life is not as it once was, where the future is in question."[26] He spoke as one who's been through this land.

Please tell me there is a path that leads out of here!

We enter this land suddenly *(meteor)*. "The tumor is malignant," "Mom, I'm pregnant," "Your mom and I are getting a divorce," "We're eliminating your position." The door to life as we know it has closed. The future is now in question. Jeff explained that the goal of his message was not to help us (me) find the nearest exit ramp out of the Land Between. *Thanks, Jeff! Not what I want to hear!* His goal was to help us *navigate* the Land Between so that when we reach the other side, our faith will have been stretched, tested, and eventually strengthened. *It's encouraging to know there is an "other side."*

While we may not have entered the Land Between by choice—perhaps even unwillingly or at least unknow-ingly—we have a choice in how we respond to the terrain of the Land. The choices we make, the actions we take in response to the challenges and tests presented to us in this Land will determine whether we exit on the other side with our faith strengthened or as a broken and bitter person.

Jeff unpacked the story of Moses in the book of Exodus. The people of Israel had been slaves in Egypt for 400 years. As they cried out to God for help, God responded by saying, "I hear your pain. I will send someone to lead you out of slavery and into a beautiful land flowing with milk and honey."[27] Moses, an Israelite who'd been adopted and raised in the home of Pharaoh, is out in the desert when he sees a burning bush. As he moves closer to investigate, he hears a voice say, "Take your sandals off your feet, for the place where you stand is holy ground" (Exodus 3:5). In this conversation, God tells Moses to go ask Pharaoh to "let My people go." The cycle of Moses asking, Pharaoh appearing to release them (only to change his mind later on), and God sending judgment is repeated several times.

Moses said to Pharaoh: "Thus says the LORD God of Israel: **'Let My people go...!'**" (Exodus 5:1). The final request for freedom culminates in God's judgment—the death of the firstborn sons of Egypt, including Pharaoh's son. Distraught, Pharaoh tells Moses to take his people and get out. There is a dramatic scene in the film *The Ten Commandments* (and in the Bible) in which Moses parts the Red Sea, and the Israelites make it across on dry ground with Pharaoh's army in hot pursuit. Then Moses raises his staff

49

as the sea comes crashing down, drowning Pharaoh's army. Pharaoh's screams of anguish are heard across the water. The door is closed. Regardless of our view of life as it once was, we will never go back there again. Now only the future is in question.[28]

You see, I like comfort. I gravitate toward routine. Predictability. I don't enjoy interruptions. Surprises. Meteors. But during my Journey through this life, I've noticed that when I get too comfortable, God shakes things up. He gets me to move out of my comfort zone and into unfamiliar territory, causing me to trust Him more. Instead of taking me directly from Point A to Point C, it seems there is this space, Point B or the Land Between, where God takes me first.

While Point C, the Promised Land, sounded pretty good to the Israelites, they weren't prepared or equipped for life in this new land. So God took them to Point B—the desert—for a season of instruction. Equipping. Preparing. This was to be a training ground designed to prove God's faithfulness and to teach Israel that they could trust God with anything that came their way. They had strayed from the God of Abraham, Isaac, and Jacob. They'd adopted much of the local culture and religion while living in Egypt, incorporating foreign thoughts and traditions into their own lives and culture. But this way of living wouldn't be acceptable to God once they were in the Promised Land. Thus, God gave the Israelites some guidelines and expectations (not to mention the Ten Commandments) to help them navigate this new land. And all of their training and preparation took place in the desert. Point B. The Land Between.

Manna (literally translated, "What is it?") was a wafer-like substance that appeared with the morning dew on the desert floor. God provided this food every morning, and it sustained the million-plus Israelites out in the desert for many years. But after a few years of desert wandering, eating only manna for breakfast, lunch, and dinner, their vision of the Promised Land started to fade. Anger. Bitterness. Talks of mutiny against Moses. Yet God still responded to their complaints and provided for their needs through Moses.

Not much time passed before the people once again forgot God's provision and constant guidance. They were caught in a never-ending cycle of crisis. Complaining, "We want REAL food!" Grumbling, "Moses, you'd better do better than this stuff. We don't even know what it is!" And then God's provision, "You want meat? I'll give you meat!"[29] Feeling the weight of the people's constant demands, Moses collapsed in a fit of anger and discouragement, possibly even depression. Paraphrasing Numbers 11, Moses said, "What have I done to you, God? Am I not doing what you asked? These people are driving me crazy. I can't stand the whining. I have had it!" Then Moses pleaded: "God, if you have any positive feelings toward me at all, then please just kill me now. Take me out! I am done! I cannot do this. I cannot do what you are asking of me. It's too hard!"

There is something about enduring a season of unremitting difficulty that clarifies one's faith.[30]

Ann

Ann and her husband have attended our church for several years. After many attempts to have a baby failed, Ann went in for a checkup. The meteor of "It's malignant" thrust them into the Land Between. Her husband, obviously devastated, hung on to hope by a thread. Given only a few months to live, Ann found herself lost in the Land Between. She and her husband bought an RV and toured the United States during Ann's final months.

I hear your pain.

Seven years passed, Ann has been holding on to God's grace and mercy every day. It helped her navigate the Land Between. But then reality caught up with her. Ann felt another growing cyst and gradually accepted the fact that her borrowed time had run its course. Living somewhere between accepting the additional unexpected years and pleading for more, she visited the doctor to confirm what she already knew...

"I'm *what?*"

"Pregnant?"

"Are you serious?"

The misdiagnosis led to the delivery of a healthy baby boy!

Sonia

Sonia was six years old, yet her life was already difficult. Having battled many disabilities, the simplest things were not so simple. Sonia's mom called the church office and asked if there was anyone who would pray with her. The doctors were going to take Sonia off life support that night. When I met with Sonia's mom, she showed me a picture of beautiful and happy Sonia at Disneyland the year before.

I hear your pain.

Sonia passed away that night. *How do I prepare to lead a memorial service for a six year old? What hope could I possibly give her family? "All things work together for good...*

Jesus loves you..." I cried out to God, *Please give me something to say to everyone who comes to the service.*

I wasn't prepared to see (or hear) more than 200 Harley-Davidson motorcycles enter the parking lot before Sonia's memorial service. Sonia's father was the leader of a motorcycle club. Let's just say this wasn't your typical Let's-go-for-a-ride-after-church bike club. I'm guessing many of these folks hadn't darkened the door of a church in a very long time. I finished my message with, "Welcome to the Land Between. God hears your pain." There wasn't a dry eye in the building. Large. Tough. Sixteen-inch blades tied to their hips.

I hear your pain.

Linda

Linda is a strong, determined single mom who attends our church with her two young children. The bills were piling up and the thought of no Christmas for the kids this year was too much. In all humility, Linda asked me if I knew of anyone in our church who'd be willing and able to adopt a family in need for the holidays. If so, "We are a family in need," She said. Tears seeped from her eyes as she tried to hold it together. Life was beginning to be too much to bear.

As I helped her get a few bills under control, some families in our church went above and beyond to provide presents for Linda and the kids. The only thing left: "Hey, Linda, my wife and I would like to invite you and the kids over for Christmas dinner."

As Linda began to open up to us, we learned that her ex-husband had committed suicide in Mexico earlier that year. "How do I tell my kids their dad isn't coming home for Christmas...ever?"

I hear your pain.

My Journey into the Desert

On the evening of November 22, 2009, after my wife told me "our son is gay" and I went upstairs and talked with him, I was feeling as though I'd just survived a meteor strike and was thrust into the Land Between. I cried that night like I'd never cried before. *Or had I? I seem to remember another time...*

Journal Entry—July 31, 1992
The pace of life has begun to increase. Rising demands at work. Preparing for a baby. *Picking up strange food items from my wife's side of the bed.* Believing that God has been calling me out of the business world and into a life of ministry, I have

been taking a full load of seminary classes. We are expecting our first child. The baby's room has been set up for months in anticipation. The matching crib, changing table, and dresser are strategically placed in the room. Animated characters dangle over the crib awaiting little eyes to focus on them for the first time. My wife and I sit next to the crib holding a stuffed animal. *Do you hear the silence?*

Somewhere during those first three months of sleeplessness after the baby was born, I remember sitting on my bed reviewing one of the papers I'd written for my ethics class. My wife sleepwalked into the room, handed me our son, and said, "Your turn! Try and get him to sleep." She smiled and exited the room. Setting down my paper on the pillow to my left, I took our son in my right arm and cradled him. Patting. Bouncing. Rocking. And all while trying to review my paper. Other guys in my class researched and wrote on topics such as the role of women in ministry or divorce. Issues that we'd have to navigate as future church leaders. But I chose to write on homosexuality—a topic that the church was currently either unwilling to address or too busy building a wall to keep "them" out. But I felt this issue could not be ignored, and building walls between God and people doesn't seem to be what serving God is supposed to be about. I felt a little frustrated with my professor's willingness to brush over this difficult, yet important issue.

Journal Entry—December, 1992

My son is drifting into a milk coma. Maybe it's my lack of sleep or maybe it's God starting to break my heart for what breaks His, but I sense a presence of God. A spiritual tap on the shoulder telling me to remember this moment. I pause. Paper in my left hand. A cooing innocent infant in my right. *This isn't a coincidence that I'm holding my paper and my son, is it? Paper. Son. Paper. Son. Paper-son. Are you trying to tell me something? My SON? MY son? God, haven't you read my paper? Most research suggests that there is little, if any, evidence of a genetic link. Rather, many psychologists suggest there is a link to an abusive or absent father! All my life, all I ever wanted to be was a daddy. Are you telling me I'm going to be an abusive father? I'm confused! We're going to go on secret missions, remember? We're going to have guy time.* I sense a stillness, a silent presence from God. It appears that God is not interested in my psychology. Or my biology. Or my ethics paper. Not even my theology.

Men: What am I supposed to do?

De: I'm not asking you to do anything.

Men: Do I tell my wife?

De: If you want to.

Men: What about my research?

De: Interesting perspective.

Men: (*Throwing the paper on the floor*) But he will have such a difficult life!

De: Difficult. Perhaps. Purposeful. Yes.

Men: (*Pleading*) Is there any other way? No Lord, please!!

A silent scream raced through my body. Tears began to flow. Gasping for air while trying not to wake my son, I buried my face in the pillows for what seemed like hours. Exhausted and empty, life must go on. But how? I will bury this premonition. Perhaps I will need to revisit this later. Thus ends the second cry.

Back to November 2009

For several months after that Sunday evening when my son confirmed his sexuality, I found myself wrestling with God. I was unable to reconcile my theology and my reality. For many years I'd enjoyed a season of closely walking with the Lord. I'd experienced Defining Moments in which God clearly spoke into my life. Over the years I'd even counseled many people who'd been hit by meteors, and it was as if God spoke through me to help them in their time of need. I felt like a vessel in God's hand, an instrument being used by the Master to accomplish His purpose. My life had meaning.

Yet now in *my* time of desperation, when I needed a whisper from God, it was as if God had gone silent. *I trust You, God. You've never left me nor forsaken me. I know I can get through this with Your help…all things are possible through Him who strengthens me.*[31] *I just need to know You're still there…Hello! …Hello? …WHERE ARE YOU?!*

Deafening silence.

Emotional Half-Pipe

I teach the third through fifth grade kids at our church, and one of my goals is to make church fun so the kids will want to come back. Growing up, I'd found church to be pretty bland...boring. *I couldn't wait for the service to be over so we could run down to the fellowship hall and get a donut.* So in order to get the kids' attention at our church, we have our third through fifth grade room set up with some games, crafts, LEGOs, and other kid stuff for them to do after their parents drop them off.

One of the things we set up last year was a Tech Deck skate park. Tech Deck is the latest thing for young boys. They're finger-sized skateboards that you can maneuver around a miniature park. We took a piece of plywood and assembled an industrial park on top of it, complete with rails, pool, mini ramp, and street scene. The most popular attraction is the half-pipe. A structure with a U-shaped cross section that lets the kids maneuver their skateboards back and forth. On the top of each side of the ramp, there's a platform where you can land your board or launch back into the pipe to get maximum speed. If I let them, kids would sit there for the entire service pushing their boards up one side of the pipe and trying to get some hang time without crashing, only to plummet back down the ramp and then up the other side.

In the middle of *my* desert, there is also a skate park; and I seem to be stuck on this emotional half-pipe. I launch myself off the top left platform, called "Anger," race down the U, and then glide up the right side only to land on "Depression." Then it's back down the ramp, careening out of control toward "Anger," and I repeat the same cycle over and over again.

Depression

In his book *Have a Little Faith*, Mitch Albom writes this about depression:

> I knew depression was real, and in many cases required medical attention. I also knew we overused the word. Much of what we called "depression" was really dissatisfaction, a result of setting a bar impossibly high or expecting treasures that we weren't willing to work for. I knew people whose unbearable source of misery was their weight, their baldness, their lack of advancement in a workplace, or

their inability to find the perfect mate, even if they themselves did not behave like one. To these people, unhappiness was a condition, an intolerable state of affairs. If pills could help, pills were taken. But pills were not going to change the fundamental problem in the construction. Wanting what you can't have. Looking for self-worth in the mirror. Layering work on top of work and still wondering why you weren't satisfied—before working some more.[32]

Sunday mornings at church seems to be a place where many parental custody hand-offs take place. Dad had the kids for a weekend of fun, trying to overcompensate for not being there during the week. ("If your mom would only lighten up.") Mom prepares for the reality of a difficult week as the kids readjust from "vacation with Dad" to "life with Mom." ("If your father would only help with some of your home-work, maybe do a load of laundry...*now there's a concept!*")

"Sorry, Pastor Chris. Their father was late *again* and didn't give them their meds...*again*! So I just dosed them up. If you see any *unusual* behavior, give me a call. I'll be in *big* church."

Unusual behavior? This happens *every* week. Depressed kids are given meds to perk them up, and angry kids are given meds to calm them down. So I spend the next hour and a half (or more, depending on how the Spirit leads in big church) feeling depressed as I watch the children caught in a parental battleground and getting angry because the service is going long...*again!* WHERE ARE MY MEDS? Oops. Sorry...where was I?

I understand there are times when medication is necessary. I get it that the service will go long more times than not. This is part of my world. Some situations in life are tensions to be lived in, not problems to be solved. Am I really going to let my frustration over the length of the church service turn into anger and then get to the point that I need medication? I don't think so! Is it okay to be angry or to get depressed? Sometimes. Just don't set up camp there!

For most of 2010, I found myself unable to get up in the mornings. Having a life driven by purpose was suddenly not enough. I needed to know how that purpose, having been altered by a meteor strike, fit within the bigger tapestry of "His" story. I don't believe God abandoned me. I don't believe I lost my salvation. I do believe God went silent in my life for whatever reason. (See the book of Job.) Where is the wonder of it all—like when I first became a believer? Even in the midst of my business going bankrupt years ago, as awful as that was, I still sensed God's ever-faithful presence helping me through difficult times. But now the place of God in my soul is blank. An interior darkness.[33]

There may be something about enduring a season of difficulty that strengthens one's faith. But if I'm honest, *enduring* doesn't sound all that attractive at the moment.

Tecate, Mexico

When I need a reality check or when I think I have it bad, I drive 45 minutes to the Mexican border, get my car insurance, pop a few of those wax covered chocolate donuts I call "vitamins," and then drive another 25 minutes to my little safe harbor- H.I.S. Ministries' Sus Angelitos Children's Center.[34] (Sus Angelitos means "His Little Angels."). Three hundred kids come through this daycare facility each day. I usually arrive to shouts of "Pastor Loco!" I guess I'm the only gringo crazy enough to drive two hours to play with a bunch of kids. Many of them don't have a father in the house...if they even have a house.

Christian is 12 years old and one of nine children in his family. I guess we connected because our names are the same: Christian, NOT Christopher. We joke about people who keep calling us Christopher. As we play soccer and I hand out candy to the kids, Christian doesn't seem to know, or care for that matter, about any of the things that are on my mind that day. He's just glad I came.

Pastor Medi is *mi amigo*! Medi works in the local brick and pottery factory making the red clay pots that you and I buy at Home Depot. *If* Medi gets paid, he might make $35 a week for more than 60 hours of work. After his *day* job, Medi tends to the people in his congregation, his neighborhood. Suddenly, my issues don't seem all that bad.

Journal Entry—March 24, 2010
Today I'm going down to Tecate, Mexico, to visit the church and daycare. It's been three years since I committed to help them put a roof on the church. Having secured the funding, it's finally happening. *Maybe I'll get something out of this trip to jar me out of this depression.* "Wazzup, Christopher? Just kidding!" The roof is progressing. It will be finished in Tecate time...mañana! Pastor Medi and I talk about the fish taco party we're going to have when the church is finished. That is, if we don't run out of money first. We converse in our own Span-glish using the few words we mutually understand. After a few awkward moments of silence, I go back to playing with the kids. Everyone knows how to speak the language of *soccer*!

I head for home feeling slightly encouraged—good enough to start down the ramp of depression on my way back toward anger.

Anger

Whenever I sense the kettle of my soul starting to boil over, I turn to Pastor Yoda. "Path to the dark side, anger is." A little warning sign goes off in my head alerting me to a potential blowout. Rather than turn away from God, I decide to lean into God.

My wife and I decided to get out of our routine, so we visited Shadow Mountain Community Church with Dr. David Jeremiah. He is known internationally, and the church isn't far from our home. We hid in the balcony and sat close to the exit. Music. *Check.* Announcements. *Check.* Everything was going smoothly so far. Then Pastor Jeremiah came on stage, and his message was on…wait for it…wait…anger! He spoke out of the book of Job. *Listening to him talk about anger was making me angry.* Here is my journal entry after that night.

Journal Entry—July 26, 2010
Last night we went to Shadow Mountain. David Jeremiah spoke on anger. Anger toward God can

be a sign of spiritual growth...it means you have realized that God is bigger than the box you have put Him in, and it's making you uncomfortable. It's okay to be angry with God. Just don't camp there. Job didn't know about the deal God had with Satan. He didn't know there was a spiritual purpose behind everything. Job just received death(s) in his family, destruction of his property, his health deteriorated— all this in the face of being obedient. *Thanks a lot!* Job had been doing everything "right." Is the grave all I have to look forward to? Where is the hope in that? God could have responded to Job's requests at anytime. However, He chose to wait. Thus Job's anger and frustration.

Then Pastor Jeremiah said the words that echoed in my head:

"Will your faith withstand God's silence?"

It's easy to have faith if God holds your hand through every crisis. But when God remains silent, will your faith stand still? Pastor Jeremiah retold a story from Philip Yancey *(paraphrasing a paraphrase)* about a friend who was swimming just off shore. Fog rolled in very quickly. Silence! No visibility. Can't see the shoreline. Panic! Moments of swimming desperately in one direction only to make a 90-degree turn and swim even harder. Stop. Tread water. Float to conserve energy. And then in the quiet he could hear a still small voice. He pointed himself in that direction and swam with everything he had.

If you are angry with God, be still. Be silent and wait for the still, small voice.

I don't hear any still small voice...the fog of discouragement and hopelessness is rolling in. God has been there too many times for me. I know my prayers have been answered in the past. My anger and frustration is at God! He is larger than the God I thought I understood. There is a bigger plan, a longer timeline, a deeper love. I don't understand it yet. I definitely do not like it.

> When I thought *how* to understand this,
> it *was* too painful for me—
> Until I went into the sanctuary of God;
> *Then* I understood their end.
> —Psalm 73:16-17

Perhaps the still small voice *is* there, buried beneath the screams of anger and the apathy of depression. Anger has a way of choking out God's voice. I will trust that God hears my pain. I will trust Him that I do not know the end and may not know it until I'm on the other side of heaven. When pain, depression, or anger is visible, let it drive me *into* the sanctuary of God, not away from it. I think God can handle my anger. At least I still recognize there is a God with whom to be angry.[35]

When God Goes Silent

I find that I gravitate toward quiet. That is probably why most of my writing takes place between the hours of 2 and 6 a.m. No phones ringing. No barking dogs. I try to write during the day, but the simplest of noises is distracting. After several hours of writing, the sun begins to rise and I hear the chirping of birds outside. That is my cue to stop typing and start my day. From the sound of the automatic coffee maker coming to life and inviting me downstairs to the sounds of the congested freeway, the average noise level has increased considerably by the time I get to work.

Have you ever reached your maximum noise level? When you just want to put yourself in time-out, close the door of your room, and enjoy a good book while leaving the rest of the world outside? Have you ever thought about your minimum noise level? Do you need one of those machines that emits white noise because it's too quiet to sleep? Most of us have spent our life within the boundaries of our own personal noise range, oblivious to the amount of noise we constantly filter out.

Deafening Quiet

At the age of 25, I decided to begin a new life in which I'd actually try to live out the faith that I now professed. For instance, I'd read through the Bible for the first time on my own. So I began reading my Bible daily and praying. Then I used my new compass to point me toward True North.[36] And I tried to put off bad habits and put on new ones. "But now you yourselves are to put off all these: anger, wrath, malice, blasphemy, filthy language out of your mouth...Put on the new *man* who is renewed in knowledge according to the image of Him who created him" (Colossians 3:8, 10).

Years later, after moving to San Diego, I took classes to study the life of Jesus. I spent a week in Death Valley to create some space for God and reduce the noise in my life so I could learn to listen to and truly hear God. It was out in the desert, hundreds of miles away from any cars, planes, or cell phones, that I heard the "deafening quiet" of the rhythm of a large bird as it pushed the air from underneath its wings. At first I thought this pterodactyl had to be right above me—it was that loud. But after searching the sky for a minute or two, I finally spotted a crow flying more than a mile away. And the clip-clop of a wild horse had to have been almost five miles away, barely visible to the naked eye. Now *that's* deafening quiet.

Deafening Silence

I often wondered what it would be like to walk with God in the cool of the afternoon. After all, this was God's initial intent.[37] For the last 15 years, I've learned that if I seek God, He promises to be found.[38] It's not quite as easy as having Him on speed dial or being able to text back and forth. It's more like trying to find the space between two local radio stations so I can plug in my iPod and listen without interference. On a long road trip, I have to readjust my iPod several times to other frequencies, or else encroaching stations will begin to drown out my iPod. (Actually, it's my son's iPod that *he* now has to adjust on the road trip back to college.)

I'm not saying I have this dialed-in relationship with God. I'm not saying God (audibly) talks with me on a regular basis. But the supposition that the Creator of the universe desires to communicate with His creation is a concept that I was pursuing. After years of drawing closer to God and hearing that still small voice, I sensed His call on my life to quit my *real* job and become a pastor.

What? That's a bit extreme, don't you think? I kind of like this getting acquainted stuff, but now You're messing with my life...I need a little more than a "feeling" to convince me it's really You!

Knowing this career change would impact my family, dramatically change the course of my life, and have lifelong, if not eternal, implications, I *really* wanted to know for sure that this was God trying to communicate with me. Early one morning as I was quietly reading my Bible and pleading with God in prayer to please show me what I was supposed to do, I came across a verse that resonated within my heart as I read it—Psalm 143:8. I paused and then I read it again:

"Cause me to hear Your lovingkindness in the morning,

For in You do I trust;

Cause me to know the way in which I should walk,

for I lift up my soul to You."

While I was sitting there pondering the gravity of getting this decision right or wrong, the phone rang. I picked it up and before I could say anything, the familiar, loud, sometimes crazy, and almost always accurate voice of a spiritual mentor of mine came to life:

"GOOD MORNING, BROTHER. PRAISE GOD! ARE YOU LOVING YOUR WIFE AS CHRIST LOVED THE CHURCH AND GAVE HIS LIFE FOR IT? I HOPE SO. I WAS PRAYING THIS MORNING AND FELT THE LORD GIVE ME A VERSE...FOR YOU. I DON'T KNOW WHAT MEANING IT HAS FOR YOU OTHER THAN I JUST NEED TO GIVE YOU THE MESSAGE. THE VERSE IS PSALM 143:8, AND IT SAYS, 'CAUSE ME TO HEAR YOUR LOVINGKINDNESS IN THE MORNING, FOR IN YOU DO I TRUST; CAUSE ME TO KNOW THE WAY IN WHICH I SHOULD WALK, FOR I LIFT UP MY SOUL TO YOU.' GOD BLESS YOU, BROTHER. HAVE A GREAT DAY." *(Click)*

That was freaky! The message was loud, clear, direct, and left no room to question. I took that as God's confirmation.

Connecting the dots between these types of Defining Moments was like finding the next piece to a puzzle. There was a good feeling of accomplishment and purpose. I had a sense of "I'm on the right track and making progress." A bigger picture was starting to emerge. Doing life with God inside that picture was beginning to find its groove. But as *they* say (whoever "they" are), "You don't know what you've got until it's gone."

"My God, My God, why have You forsaken Me?"
(Matthew 27:46)

"He has fenced up my way, so that I cannot pass;
and He has set darkness in my paths." (Job 19:8)
"He has led me and made *me* walk *in* darkness and not
in light." (Lamentations 3:2)

"I will send a famine on the land, not a famine of bread
...but of hearing the words of the LORD." (Amos 8:11)

Bible verses that I have read many times before now suddenly and painfully come to life. As Jesus was dying on the cross, in His greatest moment of need, God went silent. Other pillars of faith in the Bible (Hebrews chapter 11 lists a few) indicate that as they cried out, God seemed to turn away.

Very few would disagree that Mother Teresa was a woman who walked with God. Yet after many years of "hearing from God," she described an extremely long season of life that she called her "interior darkness"[39] or what many faiths call the "dark night of the soul."

David Seamands, in his book *Living With Your Dreams*, describes the dark night of the soul in this way:

This is the darkness which some of the saints have described as the seeming withdrawal of any feelings of God's presence from the soul. Instead, there is a strong sense of His absence. Such a time of deep spiritual aridness is called by various names: "the long dark night of the soul," "a spiritual desert," "the wilderness of the soul." It is God's discipline of darkness so that we will stop walking by sight and learn to walk by faith (2 Corinthians 5:7).[40]

Seamands goes on to explain that while communicating with God is enjoyable and rewarding, life does not cease without it. He quotes A. W. Tozer:

Feeling is the play of emotion over the will, a kind of musical accompaniment to the business of living, and while it is indeed most enjoyable to have the band play as we march to Zion, it is by no means indispensable. We can work and walk without music and if we have true faith we can walk with God without feeling.[41]

While walking with God, I suddenly find myself standing alone. I've only just realized that God has stopped. Continuing on alone, I turn and talk to the wind. Reading my Bible each morning has lost any experiential value. My prayer life has collapsed. Daily life has become labored. Words have lost their meaning.

"Love—the word—it brings nothing. I am told God loves me—and yet the reality of darkness and coldness and emptiness is so great that nothing touches my soul."
—Mother Teresa[42]

Lazarus

Jesus often traveled through Bethany, and he'd stop at the home of Mary, Martha, and their brother Lazarus. So when the two sisters realized their brother was sick and may soon die, they sent word to Jesus. After all, they'd seen Jesus heal the sick many times before. They *knew* Jesus could heal Lazarus. But time was running out. They needed Jesus to respond quickly before it was too late. As word reached Jesus and his friends, He said, "This sickness is not unto death, but for the glory of God, that the Son of God may be glorified through it" (John 11:4). Then Jesus waited until after Lazarus had died before he traveled with his disciples to Bethany.

Where is Jesus? Why hasn't he come? Lazarus died. <Silence>. Funeral arrangements were made. <Silence>. Hope was lost and still there was silence.

Several days later, Jesus arrived in town, and Mary and Martha were still grieving their brother. Martha said, "Lord, if You had been here, my brother would not have died" (John 11:21).

"I am glad for your sakes that I was not there, that you may believe" (John 11:15).

The purpose of Jesus' silence was not to intentionally cause Mary and Martha pain, although that was a natural outcome of watching their brother die. Jesus' intended (but as yet unknown) purpose was to bring glory to God. Most people in Bethany knew that Jesus could have healed Lazarus. It didn't require a lot of faith to believe that. And yet Jesus still felt their pain and wept with them—even in the midst of revealing His purpose.

Paraphrasing John 11:22-44—

"Martha, your brother will be alive again."

"I know, Jesus. We will all see him in the last days, during the resurrection."

"Martha, I AM the resurrection. I AM the life. If you believe in Me, though you may die, you will live again. And if you live and believe in Me, you shall never die. Do you believe this, Martha?"

Mary, Martha, and Jesus walked to the gravesite. By the time they got there, a crowd had gathered. Perhaps they were disappointed by Jesus' silence and the fact that He didn't get there in time. What could Jesus do now? Lazarus was dead.

Jesus asked to have the stone rolled away from the grave.

Are you sure? Lazarus has been dead for several days! It's not going to be a pretty sight, and it's going to smell pretty bad! But if you insist...!

Then Jesus called out, "Lazarus. Come out! NOW!"

With that, Lazarus came out of the grave. Alive!

Jesus said to Martha:

"You are exactly right. If I had come when you asked, your brother would not have died. You know that I could have healed him because you have seen Me heal people many times. If I had come when you asked Me to, I would have healed him. But you would have never experienced any more about Me than you already know. I knew you were ready for a greater revelation of Me than you have yet known. I wanted you to see that I am the resurrection and the life. My refusal and My silence were not rejection.

They were an opportunity for Me to disclose to you more of Me than you have ever known."[43]

Is my faith able to outlast God's silence? I am compelled that my faith can (and will) outlast this period of darkness? But only if I cling to it in the midst of the darkness.[44]

Joseph

I love the story of Joseph as told in Genesis chapters 37–50. There are some profound lessons to be gleaned from his life. For those of you who aren't familiar with him, here are the Defining Moments in Joseph's life:

1. Joseph was the favored son — 11th out of 12 sons born to Jacob who was considered to be the father of Israel. (Genesis 37)
2. Joseph received dreams or visions from God that depicted the future. These dreams included images of his family bowing down before him.
3. The dreams weren't very popular with his brothers who eventually sold Joseph into slavery and convinced Jacob of his favored son's "untimely death."

4. Joseph became a slave of a prominent man in Egypt named Potiphar. (Genesis 39) God's blessing was upon Joseph, and he prospered in all that he did. Potiphar made Joseph overseer of his entire house.

5. Potiphar's wife tried to seduce Joseph, but Joseph declined. With the anger of a spurned woman, she made up a story and had Joseph thrown in jail.

6. Years go by. Trapped in a cell, Joseph gained favor with the keeper of the prison.

7. Pharaoh had some haunting dreams, but no one could tell Pharaoh what the dreams meant.

8. Joseph was called out of prison to interpret the dreams for Pharaoh. The dreams were an economic forecast: Seven years of abundance followed by seven years of exceeding drought and blight.

9. Joseph was promoted to the highest position in the land under Pharaoh, and he developed a plan to save the people from starvation.

10. Meanwhile, Joseph's family was starving back in Canaan. Hearing there was food in Egypt,

they made the long journey to get food so they might survive.

11. Not realizing who stood before them, the brothers bowed down before Joseph and humbly requested food.

12. Joseph realized that what his brothers meant for evil, God intended for good. His dream became reality.

After being sold into slavery, Joseph made the best of his "new normal." And just when he thought things couldn't get any worse, he was thrown in prison for doing the right thing. There is something about being in the darkest, most depressed state that makes a person more capable of learning something about himself. So Joseph needed to decide if his depression would make him bitter and bent toward revenge (against his brothers) or move him toward forgiveness. Joseph went on to have his most significant impact on the world—*after* his deepest depression.

Is it possible for the best version of oneself to emerge while one passes through a season of profound disappointment, unnerving chaos, or debilitating pain?

If Joseph had known the end of the story at the very beginning, would he have willingly signed up for what was ahead? If Job or Mother Teresa had known that the outcome would ultimately exceed the cost, would they be more patient and understanding in the midst of their trials?

What if Joseph decided life wasn't going in the direction that he wanted it to and chose to take the ultimate *out*? I have come to learn that by choosing to take the early exit ramp, I miss out on the spiritual transformation that can only occur in the Land Between. Will my relationship with God be hindered, plateau, or even stagnate if I don't learn to successfully navigate this dry land?

It is far better to believe that God is out there and choosing to remain silent than to believe that no one is listening.

By no means do I consider myself equal with Jesus, the pillars of faith mentioned in the Bible, or even Mother Teresa. Yet there is some comfort in knowing that others suffering from depression have gone before me. I am starting to see there *is* a purpose. I am coming to grips with the reality that this silence is *not* God's punishment. He *hasn't* abandoned me in my time of need. Rather, this is the Father (God) letting go of the bicycle seat as His little one (me) rides away for the first time without training wheels.

There is something to be learned in the desert—without any training wheels. There are some life lessons that are not to be missed and that can only be taught in solitude. God hasn't abandoned me in the desert; He's led me to the edge of the desert and allowed me to enter it on my own. As lonely and uncomfortable as it was, it suddenly seemed unwise for me to flee the desert or scream into His silence. Realizing this is exactly where God intended me to be, it's time to "be still, and know that I *am* God" (Psalm 46:10).

Helplessness is the feeling that God is not going to use a helicopter to extract me from the desert. Hopefulness is the confidence that there is a predesigned passageway through it. It is God's desire for me not to become stagnant in my faith believing only that which I can see (Lazarus being healed). Instead, He wants me to trust in the unseen that is yet to be revealed (Lazarus being raised from the dead). Joseph did not allow the surrounding darkness of his prison cell to enter his heart.[45] Nor will I.

Stumbling Forward

Lord, No!

What does it mean when someone says one is a Christian? For many, it's an acknowledgement of Jesus as Savior. But is that the beginning or the end of the road? Romans 10:9 says that if you confess Jesus as *Lord…* you will be saved.[46] Believing is good, but so what? Even the demons believe that, yet they tremble.[47]

Being a Christ *follower* can be a bit more challenging. Rewarding, but still challenging. It makes us uncomfortable to give up control. We don't like having someone tell us what to do. We value our freedom. We see *Lord*ship as medieval, bordering on dictatorship or slavery. Yet for those who willingly become bond-servants in Christ, there is an unexplained freedom.

My purpose here is not to get into a theological discussion, but rather to point out that—as someone who is trying to actually live out what I believe—I really have no business putting these two words, *no* and *Lord*, together. Either Jesus *is* Lord, or He is not. If He *is* Lord, then how can one say no? What one does next will telegraph one's core beliefs of who God is. If you and I truly believe Jesus is Lord, then we have to leave our agenda crushed under the weight of the meteor. We have to seek out God's direction and purpose and adjust our "all" accordingly. If Jesus is Lord of my life, then "my answer must always be Yes."[48]

Strategy

Whether it's in the military, civilian, or even spiritual life, one valuable lesson we can all use is how to (1) assess our current position, (2) identify our desired destination, and then (3) determine how we will get from here to there. While the previous chapters described the events of 2010 and how I survived a meteor strike, the subsequent chapters should shed some light on the (eternal) purpose of these events. And this revelation is not just for you, the reader. I desperately want to know that my life has purpose (even if I don't understand it) and that it's not just a bunch of random events colliding at will. As events continue to unfold in the months ahead, I trust they will be in harmony with the larger orchestra.

One thing is for sure: A *meteor* is a game changer. And the rules of this post-meteor game are unclear. Going back is not an option. Staying stationary in the desert isn't looking like a good idea either. So it's time to get moving.

Current Position

The sacrifices of God *are* a broken spirit,

A broken and a contrite heart—

These, O God, you will not despise. —Psalm 51:17

I spent the first eight months of 2010 floundering. I was shaking off the dust of the meteor and gathering my senses. At least I'd survived! My thoughts shifted to my son: *What must he be going through? How was he expecting me to react? As a father? As a pastor?* Several of his gay friends had been thrown out of their homes, disowned. While I haven't given him any reason to suspect that's how I'd react, his experience is communicating otherwise. Perhaps one day this story will be told from his perspective. But for today, this book is from the dad's point of view.

While attending the Global Leadership Summit in August 2010, I realized it was the first time since the previous November that I'd felt as though God had *not* abandoned me. This silent Presence was reassuring, yet unfamiliar. I believed God heard my pain and would ultimately use this situation to further His plan, not mine. So my first decision was to determine whether I would walk away from God saying, "No thanks" or adjust my life and get on board with His plan.

God has been faithful over and over again in my life, doing things that only God can do. Just because He is silent now doesn't mean that God never existed or that He's suddenly let me down. I will choose to look for God's fingerprints in the midst of the confusion.

"And we know that all things work together for good to those who love God, to those who are the called according to *His* purpose." (Romans 8:28)

Believing that *all* things work together for good is nice — as long as *all* things are going well. But when the meteors of life hit, God's promises are just untested theories. "Without this promise, your trials and mine could feel overwhelming, and our pain could feel unbearable."[49] If you have ever experienced what Pastor Bill Hybels calls the "whisper of God," if you've ever had a Defining Moment where you knew it could only be God, then I want to encourage you to write it down. The day will come when you'll experience the deafening silence and you'll need to go back and reference these points in your life. Author Henry Blackaby calls them "spiritual markers"—moments in time when you make decisions to adjust your direction based on the unwavering knowledge that God is leading you in a particular direction.[50] It's when you "know that you know." Having experienced this many times, I align these spiritual markers and a portion of the tapestry comes into focus. A pattern emerges that begins to tell part of a story.

Below is a summarized list of my spiritual markers. I've intentionally left off some of them because while they're meaningful to me, they aren't necessary for the purpose of this discussion. *(And I'm already feeling a little exposed by putting all my "stuff" out on the table!)*

My Spiritual Markers

1985—Fork in the Road

Singing in the church choir and feeling hungover from a party the night before, I was unable to focus on the congregation without getting a massive headache. My prayer: "God, I don't need anyone to tell me I'm a hypocrite. I've grown up in the church. I believe Jesus came from heaven and died on the cross to pay for my shortcomings. Because of that, I'm going to spend eternity in heaven with You. That's great, but I need a God who is not only interested in me when I die, but also cares about me now and is willing to help me navigate life. If that's You, then I am *all in*. If that isn't You, then I'm going to stop wasting Your time and mine…I'm done with church."

1987—First Whisper

I'd read the Bible many times before—mostly out of obligation. Around this time I started reading my Bible while expecting God to somehow communicate with me, to *give me a sign*. I read a verse that seemed to stand out from the rest: "But seek first the kingdom of God and His righteousness, and all these things shall be added to you" (Matthew 6:33). While this sounded good, I wasn't sure how it would play out in *real* life. But I was willing to give it a go. My prayer: "God, my heart's desire is to fill this void of loneliness, to be married for life. No more unhealthy relationships, no divorce, no more wondering if *she* could be the right one.

Instead of (desperately) seeking to find the right one (something I've been failing miserably at), I will seek You more diligently in prayer and by reading my Bible. I will trust that You will bring the right person to me in Your timing and that You will let me know without a doubt that *this* is the right one. Amen."

1988—Love of My Life, Life of My Love

Life was going well. With my office overlooking Valley Forge Pennsylvania, I was methodically ascending the corporate ladder. I was also looking good driving my red BMW, and I'd just put a down payment on a house that was being built in the suburbs. A friend of mine from San Diego (*always good to have a connection in California!*) called me and said her sister (Laura) would be touring the East Coast and spending some time in D.C., Philadelphia, and New York. She'd be arriving in Philly via train from D.C.. "Would you mind showing her around Philly for the day and then putting her on a train to New York?" (This was long before e-mail, texting, the Internet, FAX machines, and Mapquest.) I owed my friend a few favors, so I began to work out the logistics.

Living an hour's drive outside of Philly, I wasn't familiar with how to get to the train station or how long it would take to get there. So I arrived early and wandered around the vast cavern called The Reading Terminal. Train arrivals and departures screeched over the intercom sounding more like Charlie Brown's teacher: *Whaaa wha wha whaa wha wa wah wahh.* From my position I could see down into the heart of the station. Openings on either side looked like little rat holes. Most of the people scurrying in and out seemed to know which openings were designated for going up, and which ones were for going down. After every blast from the intercom, another wave of people would scuttle out of a different hole and scamper off as if they wanted to be the first to find the cheese.

I'm out of my element. *Was it Chestnut or Walnut Street that will take us out of the city?* I don't want to embarrass myself in front of Laura. I was also mentally rehearsing a major presentation that I had to give at work. It could mean a big promotion! With eyes glazed, I stood staring off into the hollow. Another monotone blast erupted from the intercom. Another swell of people surfaced from the deep. I sensed I was being watched. As I scanned the crowd down below, I noticed a woman with the most beautiful smile. And she was heading straight toward *me*!

When people say, "God told me...," or "God said to me...," I'm usually *very* skeptical. Does God *really* talk to people today? Does God still do the burning bush thing? I'd never heard God speak, but what happened next was the closest thing to it that I have ever experienced. This is a spiritual marker that "I know that I know" God was directing me. As my eyes locked with this woman's, I felt a presence on my shoulder—almost like a father's gentle hand, ready to give me some good advice. In my head I heard the whisper: "Don't miss this. This is *the one*." And I saw this "presence" upon her.[51]

I squeezed a 30-minute conversation with God into the two minutes it took Laura to reach me. The internal conversation went something like this:

"Are you serious?! She lives in San Diego...HELLO! I live in PHILLY! So what am I supposed to say to her—'Excuse me, I know we just met, but God told me I'm going to marry you...would you mind moving from sunny San Diego to freezing Philadelphia?' *This cannot possibly work.* Shouldn't we get to know each other first? Dating is going to be rather expensive! (They hadn't invented Skype, Facebook or IM yet!) Maybe we should just skip dating! Maybe I should just quit my career and move to San Diego! That seems logical...NOT! That doesn't even sound practical. This is insane!"

By now Laura and I had exchanged pleasantries as we walked out to the car. *My newly detailed chariot will obviously impress her!* I decided to take the "scenic" way out of Philadelphia and head back toward the suburbs. *(Translation: I'm lost!)* I tried to distract Laura as I frantically looked at the street signs. (I sure could have used a GPS!) "Over there you can see William Penn standing on the building...," blah, blah, blah. I was spouting off whatever I could remember from my sixth grade essay on the founder of Pennsylvania. Then I looked up at the street sign over the next intersection and thought this had to be it. So while Laura was looking left, I made a right turn on red. Something was *very* wrong! When the light one block ahead turned green, a wave of cars advanced our way. I couldn't believe all of these drivers were going the wrong way on a one-way street. Evasive action required!

Stay cool, you don't want her to think you don't know what you're doing. After all, you do *need to impress her.*

She could be your future wife—that is, if you survive Philly traffic! Then I did what any normal person in Philly would do: I hopped the curb and drove on the sidewalk—while still showing Laura the sights! We waited for the sea of traffic to pass by, and then I gently dropped off the curb and did a U-turn to follow all the other cars going the "wrong way." New problem: We were now heading deeper into downtown. Walnut Street? Chestnut Street? I mumbled something about Philly drivers while frantically looking for the *other* "nut" street. By now Laura must have been thinking, *I found the other nut, and he's sitting right next to me!*

We eventually made it back to my apartment. That night we watched *Moonlighting* (with Bruce Willis and Cybill Shepherd) on TV. *Cue romantic music!* Could Laura really be the one? Then with eyes that penetrated my soul, she asked me, "What are you thinking? You seem to be preoccupied with something." Cue the sound of a needle scratching across the album as the romantic music comes to a sudden halt. Silence. My heart was racing. *Do I tell her? What if I'm wrong? She'll think I'm crazy. But what if I'm right? She'll probably still think I'm crazy!*

In a step of faith, I decided to tell her. No façade, no fabrication, just simple honesty. Over the next 30 minutes, I described my journey of faith. How I grew up in the church but didn't really live it. How I have a desire to be married, to settle down, to have 2.3 kids and the white picket fence and a dog...you know, the American Dream. But the harder I sought out the right person, the more I realized I was heading in the wrong direction and needed some help. I needed to *be* the right person before I *found* the right person. I explained my journey with God: How I was now trying to live out this faith-thing. I believed that if I sought God first, then He'd fulfill the desires of my heart. I don't need to pursue them. So for the last year or so, I'd been putting Him first. And I'd told God that I'm done with broken relationships and I'm waiting for Him to show me the right one. (*Here is where the train comes off the track and I lose her!*) I said, "When I saw you come up out of the train station, I believe God told me that I'm going to maeraeyr youquiruou...maahahhry youwhouoou...*(ahem)* marry you." *There! It's all out there! I'm doomed.*

Laura smiled at me again, and I knew I would pursue this woman to the ends of the earth. She began telling me a similar but different story of broken relationships and a heartache that drove her back to the God of her youth. She said that she, too, felt that we'd get married. My jaw hit the floor. Could God…would God…does God really care about the details? So in my best Philly accent, I said, "Sooo, youz wanna git marrid or whut?"

March 1988—The Move

Laura flew back to Philly again over New Year's to "meet the family," and we announced our engagement. We also discussed logistics, as somebody needed to physically move across the country. The fact that we were both willing to walk away from everything in order to make this happen confirmed that we were on the right track. My Bible reading led me to the verses in Matthew where Jesus says the kingdom of God is like a businessman seeking beautiful pearls. When he found a pearl of great price, he sold all that he had and bought this one pearl.[52] I had a great job that was on the up-and-up. I was buying a house. What could be better? Laura had one job interview in Philly, and they were willing to hire her on the spot. *Badda boom badda bing—decision made!* Laura should move. It seemed logical; it seemed wise, yet this whole "living by faith" thing had me nervous. I *really* wanted to do what God wanted and not just what I wanted. I could sure use another whisper here.

Over the next few months, I used up my personal days off from work to create some long weekends so I could fly to San Diego and be open to God possibly leading us to the West Coast. But I was hitting the wall with my job interviews. (Do you know how many people fly in from the East Coast during the winter to look for a job?) Nobody was willing to hire me until I was already committed to San Diego. The door was not only closed—it seemed to be locked. Perhaps this was another *sign* that we should stay in Philly.

While in San Diego, we met with Pastor Phil for marriage counseling. We figured this would be a good idea since we didn't really know each other. We shared about our crossroads of having to decide where to move and our desire to do what God wanted us to do. God's whisper came as Pastor Phil shared with us. He said there may be one direction that *seems* right...even logical. When you weigh out the pros and cons, the scale is tipped in one direction over the other. Yet the peace of God, which is beyond our understanding and is greater than human logic, will guard your heart and your mind in helping you come to the decision He wants you to make.[53]

As I closed my eyes and he prayed for us, I was reminded of the passage in Genesis 12 where God tells Abraham to leave his country and his father's house and go "to a land that I will show you...and I will bless you." In that moment I felt in my heart the peace that Pastor Phil had mentioned. I knew what I had to do. Then Laura and I went to the beach to ponder Pastor Phil's comments. Sitting on a picnic table and soaking up the sun, I wished I could take some sunshine back to Philly with me. It was a beautiful day. At least we were together!

Landing back in Philly, I meandered through the crowd at the airport and went to pick up my luggage. In my heart I knew what I had to do. But the cost would be great. I'd miss out on the growing-up years of my nieces and nephews. I'd miss watching Eagles football games with my grandmother. I'd miss my mother's homemade blueberry pie. I'd miss my family and all that was familiar. I grabbed my luggage and headed for the baggage claim exit. The ice on the automatic doors crackled as they slid open, and I was hit with a blast of arctic air. *Why is this such a difficult decision?*

When I arrived home, I called Laura to let her know I'd arrived safely and that I'd be purchasing a one-way ticket out of Philly ASAP! I expected her to say something like, "Let me know your flight numbers, and I'll pick you up at the airport." Instead, *she got on a plane.* She flew to Philadelphia and helped me say good-bye to all that was familiar to me. Then the two of us boarded a flight to San Diego to begin our life together. The whisper was clear; I just needed a cold nudge in the right direction.

1990–1995—The Call

Lake Murray is a small body of water near our home that reminds me of my family's vacation spot back in Pennsylvania—Lake Wallenpaupack. *Lake Wally what?* I know, but I can go to Lake Murray in the middle of winter wearing shorts and a T-shirt and walk, pray, dial into God's whisper, and discuss with Laura the issues of life. Whenever I ask Laura if she wants to walk the lake, I usually get a nervous response. More of a flinch, really, as she recalls the many previous *whispers* that have echoed over that lake.

Since we got married in 1988, I'd been working as a computer programmer at a company in San Diego. I was content and getting into some regular routines. And I was still in the process of figuring out the California freeway system.

Oh yeah, here's a little aside. During my first week in San Diego, I learned how Californians drive in the rain... they don't! I was car number seven in an eight-car pileup on the freeway. And when it happened, I was on my way to pick up Laura from her work. (I used her car during the day to interview for jobs.) As I went to exit one freeway and merge onto another one, someone up ahead panicked and hit the brakes, triggering a long line of bumper cars. After an hour or so of giving my testimony, exchanging insurance information, and watching tow trucks haul away the piles of twisted metal, I was surprised to find that Laura's car was the only one that could still be driven. Every fender was smashed, all the lights were knocked out, the side windows were broken, and I had to wrap the seatbelt over the driver's door to hold it closed while I continued on my way to pick up Laura. But it got me there!

So I showed up a *little* late, and as I rounded the corner of the parking lot, I could see Laura up ahead. She started crying as she looked at me and then at the car. (Perhaps she looked at her car and *then* at me.) "Sorry I'm late. Traffic was horrible...you folks in California don't know how to drive in the rain!" To this day I tell her I did it on purpose to see if she really loved me and would give up everything (including her car) to marry me. After all, I gave up Philly! She never did see the humor in that.

I interject this little story here to illustrate my point that just because you hear the whisper of God to *go*, that doesn't mean it will be an easy ride. There were plenty of "car wrecks" in those first few months to make me question my decision. But I "know that I know" it was the right decision!

Anyway, back to Lake Murray. I'd been taking some classes on the Bible at our church, and it was becoming a consuming fire. *Nobody ever told me the Bible said these things!* Our church offered a program called the School of Evangelism (or "School of E," for short), and I was sensing God pulling me in that direction. And so it was time for a walk around the lake with Laura to figure this out. The program met Monday through Friday mornings with a one-week hike in Death Valley and a one-month practicum that was an overseas trip designed to get you out of your comfort zone and help you share what God has shown you with someone else. *I called it Bible Boot Camp.* My employer had already denied my request to adjust my work schedule to accommodate the program. So Laura and I prayed, tabled the idea, and planned to come back to it later.

Several months later, I learned that my company was going out of business. *Perhaps this is the time for me to go to the School of E!* I began calling all of my clients to let them know that if there was anything I could help them with before I moved on, they should let me know. One client in particular suggested we meet to discuss some options. Long story made longer—they offered me a job. I explained my desire to go to this "religious" school and asked if I could adjust my schedule for a few months. Oh, and by the way, I'd need a month off for my practicum. We agreed that the month off would be without pay, and I began my new job and school.

The practicum was set for one month in the Philippines. The cost of the trip combined with a month off without pay left a big gap in our income. It was time for another walk around the lake with Laura. *I could use a whisper, God!* The next day my boss pulled me aside to discuss the "problem" that my month-without-pay was causing the company. "It appears this will set a precedent and allow people to take time off without pay at random." *I'm doomed! I already bought my plane tickets and now he's going to tell me I can't take the time off. I knew there would be a catch.* "We cannot allow you to take time off with*out* pay. So we'll have to pay you even though you haven't earned any vacation time yet. When you return, give us a few hours in overtime to make up the difference." *Definitely a whisper, a Defining Moment!*

While in the Philippines, our team visited a town that was still digging itself out after a severe earthquake the previous year. Devastation on top of poverty. We also visited Smokey Mountain, the city's garbage dump that was residence to hundreds of children who rummaged through the dump in search of food and clothing. God was beginning to break my heart for what breaks His.

I'd heard the term *reverse culture shock,* but until you've experienced it, it's rather hard to describe. After spending a month observing extreme poverty, our flight home had a connection in Hawaii. I'd be saying good-bye to my school of E team and meeting Laura for a mini vacation. We'd spend three days cruising between the islands and then four days on Kauai. As it turned out, I spent the first two days sleeping on a lounge chair next to the pool. *(We have the picture to prove it.)* I had no energy left! When I came to, I wasn't prepared for the abundance of uneaten food being wasted. After realizing that pleading with the ship's captain to send the uneaten food to the children on Smokey Mountain was futile, I knew I couldn't go back to my *normal* life. My days spent in the 9-to-5-work-a-day world would be coming to an end.

Fast-forward a couple of years: The vice president of my department was unceremoniously fired, and I found myself in the position of acting/interim vice president of information technologies. While this sounded like a good thing, I wasn't convinced I was part of the "long-term strategy" of the company. It seemed like there'd been a lot of upheaval in the organization, and perhaps I should pay attention to the winds of change. Time for another walk around Lake Murray. I was sensing a *possible* call to full-time ministry, but I was very nervous as to how that might actually work. *I know what pastors make, and it's nowhere near what I'm making now.* I found myself in need of bigger, bolder, clearer whispers. *I know you were there before, God, but now I have children. The stakes are higher. I need to be sure if you're expecting me to quit my job and become a pastor.*

I showed up for work on Monday and learned that over the weekend a midnight deal was reached to hire an executive VP over me as VP. *Are you serious?* "You have to grab talent when you see it!" "He's an 'A' player!" Let's just say I disagreed with the "A" player status, and it was clear I would be the one moving on. My initial "sensing" was confirmed.

Our company had bought out a smaller competitor earlier in the year, and part of the deal meant that the owner of that company, a bright young woman (who seemed to have it all together and had just received a lot of money for her company) became our new VP of sales. I wandered down to her office to discuss my new boss. Now, my office was located upstairs in the back with all of the techie people, while her office was on "executive row." You know, the big offices with the huge glass window, cherry wood desks, and all the bling that lets you know this person is important?

I entered her office and closed the beveled glass door behind me. As I looked out her enormous office window at the muffled buzz of worker bees doing their jobs, suddenly an unexpected whisper came to me: *She needs God. Her life is a mess.* The words were out of my mouth before I could formulate a thought: "You need God!" *Are you serious? You could get fired for talking about God in the workplace! That would be ironic. You've really lost it now!*

Before she could respond, her eyes filled with tears, and she began crying hysterically. Over the next 20 minutes, she told me how her life was all pressed and proper on the outside. "Everyone *thinks* I have it all together. But on the inside, I am lonely, I am falling apart...I desperately need God in my life." By this time the worker bees were starting to realize there's a problem with the queen bee, and we were drawing a crowd of onlookers. (Kind of like when there's an accident on the other side of the freeway, and passersby just have to rubberneck to see what's going on.) Our session ended with her asking me to pray for her, and I walked out of her office thinking, *Now that was a Defining Moment.*

Two weeks later I sat in a room with 19 other people being "downsized." They brought in some expert to help us cope with the grief and the unexpected loss. *Whatever!* I couldn't ignore the obviousness of God's hand in my life, orchestrating circumstances to move me more in line with His purpose. I had no idea what lay ahead. I only knew that God was leading this train ride, and I was hitching my caboose. *WOOHOO!*

1996–2000—Helping God

I became more involved in our church, and I actually went on staff part-time as an associate pastor. I was glad for the opportunity to be in ministry, but the 60 percent cut in pay wasn't going to work for very long. Without wanting to be a burden to the church, I decided to *help God out.* I remembered a whisper from several years earlier—when I thought God might be leading me into full-time ministry, but I'd been unsure how to proceed. So I met with an older pastor friend who said, "Chris, if you can do anything else, if you have any talents, any desires to do anything besides ministry, do it. But once God closes that door, go into ministry and know that you can never go back." I'd always wanted to have my own business, so now seemed as good a time as any. Perhaps I could get it started and then hand if off to someone else to manage while I became a "pastor."

The business grew quickly during its first year of operation in 1996. Daily I received $50,000 checks from potential investors hoping to "get in" on the deal. At one point we had almost 100 employees and more than 400 investors. Three years into it, there were rumors of a buyout offer that would make my slice of the pie worth several million dollars. Then almost overnight, buyout rumors were replaced by lawsuits. This rocket was out of fuel and gravity soon outpaced momentum leading to a mighty crash—a bankruptcy in 2000.

As difficult as that last year turned out to be, I "know that I know" that God was in it, guiding me in making some difficult decisions. But the underlying whisper was, *What are you doing? What part of "go into full-time ministry" did you not understand? Do you not remember Matthew 6:33?* That door slammed shut. That whisper really hurt. Many people lost their jobs. Hundreds of investors, including family members, lost a lot of money. My intentions were good, but many people got hurt. *You now have my undivided attention!*

2003—Come Over Here

Our family began attending Journey Community Church (www.journeycom.org) as a preparation ground for going overseas as missionaries. I sensed the winds of change again. Another walk around Lake Murray was necessary for Laura and I so we could discuss this "heart for missions" I was feeling. How can we help people with genuine needs? There are a lot of people in the world who are hurting. I contacted Journey's senior pastor, an acquaintance of mine, to let him know we were attending Journey. I also said that if there was anything we could do to help out before we left for the mission field, please let us know. Next thing I knew, I was being offered a job as the children's pastor. While I love kids, this didn't seem to be the next logical step. I needed another whisper.

"Shepherd the flock of God which is among you, serving as overseers, not by compulsion but willingly, not for dishonest gain but eagerly; nor as being lords over those entrusted to you, but being examples to the flock." (1 Peter 5:2-3)

I felt that my calling to Journey Church was to *shepherd* and that those currently *entrusted to me* were the children (with "shepherding" being the active imperative; the children and their families being the mission field). I've now served as children's pastor at Journey for more than seven years.

I realize I could have just *listed* these Defining Moments or these whispers as bullet items and made this chapter a lot shorter. But writing this out was therapeutic for me, part of my stumbling forward. This is one of the tools I used to get off the emotional half-pipe. My mind kept coming back to one thing: My son's sexuality. For too long, I'd allowed this one issue to dominate my life and my thoughts. God had apparently gone silent leaving a void that was being filled with this one issue. Even I know that's not healthy. There is so much more to life. There is so much more to my relationship with my son.

I started this chapter with a bulleted list, recounting the moments in time when I *knew* God was there. In seeing such a long list, how could I ever doubt? Did God just abandon me? Does God even exist? Was all of this just part of my imagination? Seeing my list helped me realize that God is still God and I am not. I've enjoyed a long season of walking with the Lord. I cannot force God to communicate with me. If God has gone silent, then there must be a reason for it even if I don't (yet) understand what that is. This is where faith kicks in and determines how I proceed. But writing these stories has made me realize just how much God *does* want to be active in my life. Reliving these stories with my wife has made me fall in love with her all over again. They've melted my anger and allowed love to spring forth again. They've peeled off the depression to reveal true joy.

I've also realized that my faith in God had become dependent upon hearing His voice, seeing His leading, knowing His prompting. I'd put God inside this convenient box while thinking I understood how God works and that nothing would change. I'd developed my routine of going to God, sensing God respond in a familiar way, and my responding (hopefully, mostly) in an appropriate manner. I was settled into a comfortable life routine with God helping me pedal and occasionally suggesting we take a turn up ahead. Somehow I keep finding myself back in the driver's seat, and then I feel a tap on my shoulder and hear those familiar words: "Mind if I steer?" It gives me hope that God has not dropped me. He is not silent because He cannot find me or is no longer interested in me. Rather, His silence is intentional and meant for my good, which is in the process of being revealed. Be patient.

Shepherding was my last spiritual marker, so I will cling to that. As God's purpose begins to come in focus, I expect shepherding will play a big part in my next move. I will align my life more in tune with His plan. My list of spiritual markers reassures me that God is faithful. The next step is to do a "practical issues" inventory, which is similar to a collateral damage assessment. What are the areas in my life that need attention? And what can I do to start making some progress?

Issues Inventory

Communication with God

My lines of communication with God seem to be down. If I believe God has *intentionally* gone silent, then how can I *make* God speak to me? I am resigned that God will speak when He is ready. However, I do believe that I must do the best I can to prepare myself, so that if and when God reveals Himself to me, I'll be listening with both ears. I am also aware of the possibility that God is still speaking but perhaps I'm (a) not liking what I'm hearing and therefore practicing selective hearing, or (b) prevented from hearing God because of my anger and my frustration with Him.

I keep hearing the question in my head, *Is my faith strong enough to outlast God's silence?* My faith has done me well so far. But if I'm honest with myself, I must admit that I've been in maintenance mode. Strong, but holding steady. Teaching Bible stories to third through fifth graders hasn't required me to study the Bible very deeply for several years now. Being smarter than a fifth grader is not all that difficult. I've been able to skate along unchallenged. While my faith is strong, it's becoming obvious that it's not strong enough to take me on this next lap in my life. I need to get out of maintenance mode and get back into muscle-building mode.

Rules of Engagement

How do I approach my son in discussing this issue? We're both conflict avoiders. Both of us are able to stare right at the elephant in the room and pretend it doesn't exist. Ignoring the issue isn't going to make it go away. In our conversations I've realized that my words are being translated into something different than what I actually mean. I guess it's kind of like telling my parents in the '60s what *groovy* and *far-out* meant. We need to come up with some common vocabulary terms, as well as some parameters on how and when to discuss this issue. As I said before, there is more to life than this one issue. I really don't want us to get bogged down and only talk about sexuality. I don't want him to think that every time he comes home from college, I'm going to barrage him with questions. Yet at the same time, I want him to know that I care about him and I want to help him navigate *all* of life. Avoiding the difficult issues isn't helpful to anybody.

I do a lot of counseling, and one of the main issues that comes up over and over again is communication (or a lack of it). People have a hard time understanding each other. So here I am—a counselor in need of my own advice. One of the things I tell people is that if you want to communicate with someone, it's up to you to find out what frequency that person's receiver is dialed into, and then you need to transmit your message at the same wavelength. Just because you rattle off a bunch of words, you can't assume the other person received the message, much less understood it.

Over the past year, I've tried discussing this issue in person with my son, over the phone, and even in e-mails, and there appears to be some resistance. Instead of forcing the issue, I paused and realized that his main form of communication these days is texting. So here's how we started the dialogue almost a year later. These are my initial texts and his replies:

Txt: U said b4 u came home that u wanted to talk about being gay? Do u still want to talk?

Reply: I didn't mean we had to talk, I just don't want it to be an issue that is ignored.

Txt: But if we don't talk about it, isn't that like ignoring it?

Reply: Yes

Txt: Then I don't understand, do u want to talk about it or do u want me to leave u alone?

Reply: I don't know.

Reply: I am sure that is a frustrating response. But it is true.

Txt: Given both our personalities we would both ignore it. I think it would be healthy for us to at least try and have an open dialogue.

Ignorance

Whatever happened to investigative reporting? It used to be that when news happened, a reporter went out to get the facts. If there was a conflict, the reporter presented both sides of the argument. I don't mind a journalist sharing his opinion as to who was right or wrong—or even what he believes should be done to bring about justice. What I do mind is when a story is brushed with biased paint while I'm being told that it's a fair and balanced report. Everyone has a bias. I'd just like to know the author's bias when I'm reading an article.

I recognize *my* bias. I was raised in a conservative home, and the more I study the Bible, the more I believe it to be truth. I'm not afraid to examine problems against the filter of the Bible. Each time I wrestle with difficult issues, I'm compelled to go back to the Scriptures and reexamine my beliefs and values. I recognize that I'm not an authority on every concern; and regarding some matters, I may have a wrong belief or opinion. But if I am wrong (on any issue), I'd want to know about it. I'm also open to God doing something new. My tradition and culture tell me this probably isn't going to happen, but my conflict-avoider personality would love to have God step in and just tell me everything is okay.

I think of the story in Acts 10. Cornelius was a "good man" but not a Jew. One day he received a vision from God telling him to go find a man named Peter and bring him to his house. First off, the culture and tradition of the time was that God spoke through the people of Israel. What was God doing appearing to this Gentile "dog"? The next day, Peter received a vision. He saw a sheet coming down from heaven, and inside the sheet were animals that the Jews weren't permitted to eat. Then a voice from heaven told Peter to "kill and eat." Peter declined because the "law" (Scripture) said it was wrong. The voice spoke to Peter a second time, "What God has cleansed you must not call common (unclean)" (Acts 10:15). This scenario was repeated three times. *I guess Peter really needed to "get it."* Peter didn't understand the implications of this vision until Cornelius' messengers came knocking at the door and invited him to the Gentile's house (which was also against the law). Peter eventually made the association and realized God was doing something new. What used to be "wrong" was now okay.

I am open to God giving me a vision and telling me the issue of homosexuality isn't an issue any longer. Whether I agree or disagree with the issue or God's decision, eventually I have to conclude that I am not God. I am not the Rule Maker nor the Rule Changer. So far I haven't received any such vision, so I have to go back to Scripture and wrestle with God. Part of the debate on whether the issue of homosexuality is right or wrong is the issue of how we interpret Scripture. Why do we say that some portions of the law (eating bacon, women keeping their heads covered during church, and so on) are now okay, while others are *forever* forbidden?

I am also becoming aware of my ignorance of the great divide that this issue has caused in Christian culture. Battle lines between churches seem to be forming around this issue. Here in California, Prop 8 has become a wedge between not only the church and the GLBT community, but also between different churches. "Where does *your* church stand on Prop 8?" People may decide whether or not to fellowship together based on a political proposition.

I am suddenly aware of many parachurch organizations' versions of how to equip the church to handle the "struggling homosexual," offering help to those who want to "change their behavior." Can one change? Should one change? *Inborn behavior. Orientation. Reparative Therapy.* A year ago, these were terms I didn't know, much less care about. What does the church have to offer the GLBT community? What is the church doing to reach out and show the love of Christ to them?

The Great Commission has always led the church toward figuring out ways to take the Good News of God to people who haven't heard it yet.[54] Huge amounts of resources have been spent to identify people groups and learn their cultures and their languages. We're willing to send missionaries to the remotest jungles of the earth, yet it appears the church is unwilling to enter the part of town that flies a rainbow flag. I am quickly realizing that "the issue" is not the issue. "The issue" is actually people. *Lord, break my heart for what breaks Yours.* I need to begin putting faces on the issue. I need to make friends with people from a culture I don't yet understand.

Focus

Have you ever done a 1,000-piece puzzle in which 90 percent of the puzzle is blue sky? All the pieces look alike, and you spend hours on what looks like minimal progress. Frustration and hopelessness soon set in.

That is how my life currently feels.

There are so many pieces to my life's puzzle, yet right now everything blurs together. Few of the pieces seem to fit together. I'm even having difficulty grouping pieces with similar shades of blue. Therefore, I've taken my journaling to a whole new level of detail, trying to make sense of all these apparently random thoughts.

Community

I'm sure we aren't the only parents who've experienced this. There must be some books written by other parents who are "out there on the dance floor of life, doing the lost-parent shuffle."[55] In this era of support groups, surely there must be *something* in our area—a safe place where we can meet and talk with other parents and ask them how to move ahead. I think that's part of what the Christian experience is all about: Locking arms with someone who's a step ahead of you and following in their footsteps, while at the same time looking behind you because someone else will be coming up to stand in the same spot where you were standing just moments ago.

The Job Factor

"And the LORD restored Job's losses
when he prayed for his friends.
Indeed the LORD gave Job twice as much as
he had before." (Job 42:10)

I am aware that this is not a Bible recipe—that if I just do "this," then God is obligated to do "that." But I do believe there is something here for us (me). Basically, that healing, restoration, and progress won't be made until I get my focus off of myself and on to someone else. In reality, there are people in this world with issues more pressing than mine — some are even life threatening. Sometimes it helps if we focus on something or someone else in order to bring clarity to our issue *de jour*.

The God Whisperer

My prayers so far have been focused on "Why has God abandoned me?" I need to shift my prayers to that of anticipation. Will God reveal Himself to me again? When? How? What if I don't like what He has to say to me? This is probably one of those "Is the glass half empty or half full?" questions. Like Elijah, I am listening for that still, small voice.

Intended Destination

Create in me a clean heart, O God, And renew a

steadfast spirit within me.

Do not cast me away from Your presence, And do

not take away Your Holy Spirit from me.

Restore to me the joy of Your salvation, And uphold

me by Your generous Spirit.

—Psalm 51:10-12

While sitting with a friend the other day, I whined about how I felt abandoned by God and how He wasn't answering my prayers. Without hesitation my friend looked me in the eye and said, "Chris, what do you want God to do? 'Heal' your son? Do you want God to make your son heterosexual? Do you really believe that would make everything okay? If your son were 'normal' and got his girlfriend pregnant, would that somehow be better? While culturally that might be more acceptable and definitely more common- place, it's no less 'sinful' in God's eyes. It's also no *more* sinful in His eyes than the other [sins] listed in the Bible that the church and Christians seem willing to [overlook] today! You need to figure out your goal [*destination*]."

So my first goal was to realize that *my* goal is irrelevant. The real question is, *What is God's goal or plan for my son? For me?* I don't know God's goal for Seth. But my having a goal to *change* my son's sexuality could possibly thwart God's plan for Seth's life. Needless to say, that matter will have to be worked out between God and Seth. I may have a part in how it plays out, but ultimately it's not my issue.

What is God's goal for *my* life? What is God's desired destination for me? It's not so much a place as it is an action. If I truly believe there is a Creator God who has visited me at each of my Defining Moments, then I have to believe that God will ask me to move in the direction of faith and adjust my life plan to align better with His intended destination for me. These life adjustments set the stage for me to be obe- dient to God's next whisper.[56] Going back to Egypt is not an option. A season in the desert is under way. If I'm to continue on with God, then I'll have to adjust my life according to His plan and be willing and obedient to follow in a new and uncharted direction.

> "Get out of your country,
> From your family
> And from your father's house,
> To a land that I will show you." (Genesis 12:1)

God had a plan for Abram. God promised that he would have descendents more numerous than the stars in the sky.[57] Abram needed to adjust his life, leave everything that was familiar to him—his family, friends, and community—and go to a land "that I *will* show you." God did not tell him where this land would be, nor did He define the destination ahead of time. God said only that Abram needed to get on the path and start moving. The destination was already determined, but it wasn't yet revealed. It appears to me that God wanted Abram to remain focused on the Journey, not the destination. Therefore, I'm also going to spend less time focusing on the destination and more time studying the path.

"Behold, I will do a new thing…

Shall you not know it?

I will even make a road in the wilderness

And rivers in the desert." (Isaiah 43:19)

What new things does God want to do in the desert? God's power is sufficient to do everything and anything. He doesn't need my help to run the universe.[58] God's love draws me into not only a desire to adjust my life so it's in line with His purpose, but also a co-labor relationship with Him.[59]

What if the meteor is God's invitation and the desert is God's training ground to equip us to observe and participate in specific movements of God? When we become co-laborers with the Creator of the universe, it cannot help but draw us into a closer relationship with Him and a deeper understanding of His love for all of creation. The very place we desperately seek to avoid is the same place where God is planning on doing a new thing. Wouldn't you want to know?

The Path

"You will show me the path of life;

In Your presence is fullness of joy;

At Your right hand are pleasures forevermore."

—Psalm 16:11

"Your word is a lamp to my feet

And a light to my path." —Psalm 119:105

"When my spirit was overwhelmed within me,

Then You knew my path." —Psalm 142:3a

"Cause me to hear Your lovingkindness in

the morning,

For in You do I trust;

Cause me to know the way in which I should walk,

For I lift up my soul to You. —Psalm 143:8

My list of issues may not be complete, but I've come to the place where I am exhausted. So I will take my list, such as it is, and begin seeking God on each item and developing an action plan or a to-do list. (This is very much a Beaver personality trait.)[60] My personality would prefer to just skip ahead to the destination. However, I'm not certain that I will *ever* arrive, and I'm becoming increasingly aware that the goal *is* the Journey. The Journey of a Thousand Miles begins with the first step(s), and so here they are.[61] At the end of each step, I've paused to reflect how it's played out over the past year. On some things I've made visible progress. But on others…well…not so much.

Communication with God

Reducing the noise level in my life seemed like a good place to start. *Easier said than done!* It's time to simplify the areas of life that I do (or at least *think* I do) have control over. If I am to survive in the desert, then I need to let go of all of this "important stuff" that I'm carrying. I've noticed in the past that God seems to communicate with me the most when

I am quiet...still...alone. I think back to my time in Death Valley and my weekly treks up Cowles Mountain (a kind of mini desert experience without leaving town). So I committed to climb Cowles at least three times a week. I need to get away for short bursts, as well as for a long weekend or maybe even a week. The purpose is to seek out solitude with God.

As a pastor, I find that while people often come to me for prayer, it's difficult for me to ask others to pray for me. Perhaps I'm being selfish. Perhaps I should ask for prayer for my son. But most people who *say* they'll pray for you at church on Sunday mornings don't follow through. And I'm concerned that people might respond the way Job's friends did—"helping" by pointing out all of the problems (sins) in my life. I'm not looking for someone to "fix" me or my son—just pray. I need people who will call me at random times and say, "BROTHER CHRIS, I'VE BEEN PRAYING FOR YOU, AND..."

I realized that other things in my world might be hindering my prayer life. So I decided to give my accountability group (the Saturday Cowles Mountain hiking group) the freedom to speak into my life. I am grateful to these men. They know most of my spiritual markers, they know my heart, and they've earned the right to ask me the tough questions and keep me honest. These are go-to guys I can trust to keep my "stuff" on the mountain and tell me when I'm in the wrong. When these guys say they are praying for me, they mean it.

My desire is to get back to the basics of building my faith muscles. Creating margins on the pages of life requires increasing diligence in today's instant-access world. Turning off the cell phone, e-mail, and IM seemed like a good place to start. I also decided to carve out a little extra time in the mornings, after the rest of the family has gone their own way, to pray and just be still. But in doing that, I've come to realize just how early and how often our landline phone rings *every* day with a barrage of callers who want to sell me something or ask my opinion on this candidate or that proposition. Step One: Never answer the landline again. (I couldn't tell you the last time someone called to talk to *me* on that line.) Step Two: Unbundle the Internet and landline services and then drop the landline altogether.

I think I've done well at creating a little extra time of solitude each day. But as I write this, it's 4 a.m. and I still find myself easily distracted. For some reason I feel compelled to check Facebook on a minute-by-minute basis. Seriously, who's up at this hour anyway? During the first few months, I carved out some three-hour chunks of time here and there to go to the beach and just write in my journal and read my Bible. To be honest, I've since dropped the ball on that one. And as for getting away for a multi-day retreat, it hasn't happened yet. I've heard from several of my accountability partners, as well as my son, that I need to make that a priority.

Rules of Engagement

This was (and is) a difficult one for me. Although I exhibit the Beaver's "get-it-done" qualities at times, my dominant personality trait is the Golden Retriever or "faithful companion." Thus, I can't sleep at night knowing there *might* be a perceived issue causing stress or tension in a relationship—especially when it's a close family member. I spent most of the early months of 2010 in conflict-avoidance mode. While this may give the false appearance of peace and tranquility on the outside, on the inside everything is churning. The elephant in the room was getting bigger and harder to overlook.

I fumbled every effort to communicate with Seth by unintentionally using words with mixed meanings. I was unable to communicate my thoughts in a broader context, which led to wrong assumptions and just seemed to make matters worse. Several times I felt defeated and ready to give up. I remember one particular conversation with my son that just couldn't seem to gain any traction. And then he blurted out, "I can never win a theological debate with you…!" Suddenly it clicked! He was seeing me wearing my pastor-hat. My years spent studying the Bible were bearing down on an 18 year old who was simply trying to reconcile his theology with his present reality. The pastor-hat had become a barrier to a young man who needed to see the father-hat. Better yet, the daddy-hat. Or even better yet, the Unconditional-Dad-hat. I needed to reaffirm for Seth that I am his dad first and foremost. A temporary boundary in our conversations is implemented: No more theology unless he brings it up.

There was another time when I felt it was necessary to communicate with my son about a particular issue via e-mail. Looking back, I believe that conversation only served to reaffirm that my love for Seth is unconditional…except for this one thing: I wasn't ready for him to bring home any "friends" from college. When I brought home friends from college, we'd all crash in my parents' living room or on the floor of my bedroom. But when I brought home a girlfriend, it was different. We definitely stayed in separate rooms, we had to watch the amount of PDAs (Public Displays of Affection), and so on. How was this going to work with Seth? My discomfort quickly turned into fear. And as a result, I e-mailed Seth this long list of "conditions" that would have to be agreed upon before he brought someone home.

During our drive back to college one weekend, I apologized to Seth for building that wall of conditions. I said I didn't want to make him or his friends feel unwelcome in our home—that wasn't my intent. I suggested he just throw away that list, and we'd figure out any logistics when he came home. I said, "You and your friends are always welcome in our home." While this conversation relieved some of the tension between my son and me, I could feel an internal question starting to rise, and I'm still not sure how to resolve it. There is now a tension (perhaps a healthy tension) between unconditional love and setting proper boundaries. If he were heterosexual and bringing home a girlfriend, there's no doubt we'd establish healthy boundaries for their visit, and I don't believe the conversation would be met with such angst. So where I think I went off track was in creating a list of conditions simply to protect my fear, rather than provide healthy relational boundaries.

January 2011. My son texted me to say he was coming home for the weekend, and he was looking forward to us going out for a burrito. *(Uh oh, I think this is equivalent to my asking my wife to walk Lake Murray.)* For almost two hours, Seth and I had our best conversation in a long time. He mentioned how college has exposed him to an infinite spectrum of religious beliefs—of which Christianity is only one part. And he's also learned that people's interpretations of Scripture—even within Christianity—vary from one extreme to another on a whole host of issues. What he thought was a nice, neat box labeled CHRISTIANITY now appears to be challenging his own distinct borders, creating grey space in a black-and-white world. And it's drawing him back into the Bible to more deeply understand or confirm his beliefs. God has outgrown the box in which my son had put Him. (My words, not his.)

Seth also talked about a friend from school that he was concerned about. After several conversations regarding family and faith, this young man explained how he'd immigrated to the United States a few years after he witnessed his parents' murders. My son found it difficult to navigate his friend's anger and bitterness toward God. "How do you explain a loving God in the midst of tragedy?" As Seth described the situation, my heart went out to this young man. *(Lord, break my heart for what breaks Yours.)* Seth's friend is rejecting the very source of comfort he so desperately needs. I also realized he had the potential of becoming more than a "friend" to my son. But the issue of his relationship with God far outweighs any discomfort I might envision. My heart truly is broken for this young man.

Ignorance

I've never been much of a student. I'd much rather watch a movie than read a book. *(That's probably why all of my teaching analogies come from animated movies.)* But this issue of homosexuality and how God wants me to respond has become a consuming fire for me. Mastering the art of one-click shopping on Amazon, I now own an entire shelf full of books that I've simply devoured. (If you're interested, check out the bibliography for a list of the ones that have impacted me the most during this Journey.) Some books were lifesavers; others were a big disappointment.

I've read more than 30 books in the last six months, which amazes even me! But I quickly realized that I've barely scratched the surface. I'm only discovering how truly ignorant I really am. And I do recognize my bias, as most of the books I've purchased are Christian based. So one of my goals for 2011 is to learn more about this issue from outside the Christian filter. I need to make sure my research is *fair and balanced*. But my ignorance is not limited to the GLBT community at large; I'm also lacking when it comes to rightly discerning the Word of God. I need to go back into the Scripture and reexamine how I look at, study, and apply God's Word to my life.

One of the difficulties that I see in the Christian community is this attitude of "God said it, I believe it, that settles it." *I have to admit, that used to be me.* It's the idea that if it's in the Bible, then that's the way it is. Many conservative Christians interpret the entire Bible literally. So when someone from the GLBT community encounters a "Christian," instead of seeing the unconditional love of God, they see a list of conditions. They see the Christian community putting up barricades or boundaries, such as Prop 8, to keep "us" in and "them" out. When Christians behave that way, is that honoring biblical commands?

Why is it that most Christians can quote John 3:16 ("For God so loved the world that He gave His only begotten Son, that whoever believes in Him should not perish but have everlasting life.") and only the first half of Leviticus 20:13

("If a man lies with a male as he lies with a woman, both of them have committed an abomination...."), while the GLBT community knows the entire verse of Leviticus 20:13 *("... They shall surely be put to death. Their blood shall be upon them.")* but doesn't know John 3:16?

Just this week in Uganda, a "Christian" leader paid to have the first part of Leviticus 20:13 printed in a newspaper: "If a man lies with a male as he lies with a woman, both of them have committed an abomination." Yet when a gang went out and murdered a young man because he was gay, this Christian leader started back-pedaling, saying that wasn't what he meant. Well, that *was* what he meant if he's in the camp that translates the entire Bible literally, because the rest of that verse says, "They shall surely be put to death. Their blood shall be upon them." Words are meaningful. If you're going to claim the high road of literal, moral self-righteousness, then be careful where that takes you.

Christians at large like to quote the first half of Leviticus 20:13 to gays as an *everlasting* judgment or mandate from God. But most Christians would agree that the second part— putting them to death—is something we shouldn't do. "That was then...this is now." So we pick and choose which verses to take literally and which are okay to discard. My point is not to say that we should never pick and choose; rather, we must recognize that *all* of us already do this. Our assertion that we don't do it isn't fooling anyone but ourselves.

> "These six things, the Lord hates, Yes, seven are an *abomination* to Him: A proud look, A lying tongue, Hands that shed innocent blood, A heart that devises wicked plans, Feet that are swift in running to evil, A false witness who speaks lies, And one who sows discord among brethren." (Proverbs 6:16-19)

> "Now the [religious leaders], who were lovers of money, also heard all these things, and they derided Him. And [Jesus] said to them, 'You are those who justify yourselves before men, but God knows your hearts. For what is highly esteemed among men is an *abomination* in the sight of God.'" (Luke 16:14-15)

Just two verses later, in verse 18, Jesus says that those who divorce and remarry have committed adultery. Now, He doesn't use *abomination* here, but the implication is that this isn't pleasing before God. What about tithing, foot washing, and surrendering *all* of our possessions? These are just a few examples of things we're told to do in the New Testament, but those practices are overlooked in many churches today. Should we then murder everyone who commits "abominations" before God? If so, then our churches would be *very* empty.

So how do we interpret Scripture? What is the process for determining which verses to take literally and which verses to ignore? The question is not *should* we pick and choose (we all do). The question is, can we pick and choose in a way that "honors God and embraces the Bible as God's Word for all times?"[62] A must-read book on this issue is *The Blue Parakeet* by Scot McKnight. In his book he uses women in ministry as an example of how churches or denominations pick and choose verses to support or deny their position. While this may be less explosive than the issue of homosexuality, it has become divisive in the church nonetheless.

In admitting my own bias, most of my spiritual growth has taken place within a denomination that exhibited a lot of grace toward the hippie movement of the '60s and '70s, yet was very adamant (literal interpretation of Scripture) about not allowing women to serve as pastors. I hadn't researched it much, as it wasn't a life-or-death issue for me. But there were women in my seminary classes, so I was intrigued as to how that was going to play out for them. I was becoming aware that not all denominations held our "right" interpretation of Scripture.

This became an issue for our congregation in 2010, as we have a very talented young woman who was hired as "director" of our college ministry. *She was actually serving as a pastor. But as long as we called her "director," somehow it was okay.* She gave the message one Sunday morning, and at the beginning of her talk, up on the big video screen popped the subtitle "pastor." Talk about the *stuff* hitting the fan! I was surprised that many whom I thought were mature believers left the church over this matter—and several were unwilling to even discuss the issue. I wasn't discounting or even disagreeing with their belief or opinion. In fact, I never even got to share my beliefs or the process God had been taking me through in dealing with this issue. I'd gone back to the Scriptures. I'd taken a more in-depth look. And my study told me that the issue is not as black-and-white as I'd made it out to be. I am trying to remain teachable as my theology on this topic is shifting.

But I believe my still-limited view of God has outgrown the box in which I'd placed Him.

While I want to have a "right" view or interpretation of Scripture, what good is it if I don't apply it? Don't get me wrong, my goal in life is not to figure out all of the rights and wrongs of the Bible and live accordingly. I already know I'm not able to do that which I know to be right (Romans 7:18-19). That's why I need a Savior! The whole point of the Bible is to draw us into a relationship with our Creator.[63] There are many well-meaning Christians who want to out-legislate pro-gay bills in the senate, who are unwilling to cultivate friendships that will help people from the GLBT community draw closer to their Maker.[64]

To be honest, women in ministry hadn't been an issue for me and my church ministry. (Most third through fifth graders don't really get into these kinds of issues.) I was comfortable teaching *safe* Bible stories to the kids. Parents like us to teach the children to obey their parents, and they prefer we stay away from any issues that might initiate uncomfortable conversations at the dinner table. But now that the issue of women in ministry is up front for our congregation, it forced me to go back to Scripture and wrestle with God some more. Now that the issue of homosexuality has hit home, I am coming to grips with my own ignorance and previous indifference, and I'm realizing that I have to go back and wrestle with God on this issue, too.

The only problem with wrestling with God is that I usually walk away limping.[65]

Focus

I started a journal for each of my sons on the day my wife informed me *we* were pregnant. My goal was to write about life as it happened, knowing that if we didn't, much of life would be forgotten. On each son's 18th birthday, he'll receive several spiral-bound journals rubber banded together to keep the pages from falling out. And now I am so thankful for the computer and the fact that I don't have to hand-write my thoughts anymore! Other than climbing Cowles Mountain, journaling has been my best tool to remain focused. If this book were a handwritten journal, part of me believes the volume of paper would reach the ceiling. Another part of me knows that if I'd had to write this out by hand, I never would have started.

During the month of January 2011, I read my 2010 journal many times. In fact, much of this book is just a reformatting of my journal, pulling together themes that came up over and over, day after day, page after page. And as I looked at all of the chaos of my random thoughts, I began to see the hand of God in the midst of all of it. Pieces of the puzzle with no defining shape started coming into focus and snapping into place. While I still don't see the larger picture *(I sure wish I had the puzzle box cover to use as a template!)*, I'm beginning to see that at least there *is* a picture. Organization is sprouting through the chaos. Randomness is being replaced with purpose.

I believe the other necessary element here is time, which helps put things into proper perspective. Focus is still an issue for me. Time does not necessarily heal all wounds. There are still days when I just can't seem to pull it together. And this is probably the main reason why I'm turning my journal into a book: It's causing me to focus on a higher level and for an extended period of time. It's creating a sense of purpose and a reason to get up in the morning.

Community

I know I need it, but why is community such a difficult issue for most men? It seems like guys need a project to tackle together before they can begin talking about anything beyond sports. My wife gets all the credit here. She attended several groups in our area (without me) so she could meet and talk with anyone who'd listen and might be willing to help us. She was learning as much as she could. She brought home books by Barbara Johnson, the author of *Where Does a Mother Go to Resign?* Barbara experienced multiple tragedies in her life prior to her son's admission that he's gay. Yet she tells her life story in a light, almost humorous tone. While I appreciated her insights, I wanted to read books written from the dad's perspective. In fact, the more I read, the more I felt condemned by the "cause" of homosexuality being described as the result of an absent or abusive father.

My wife began attending a small group at a church nearby, and she went for several months before I mustered enough courage to go with her. I was embarrassed. Ashamed. Fearful. After all, this particular church took a high-profile position on Prop 8. And as a result, their pastor has taken a lot of heat from the GLBT community as being anti-gay. But it was through his leadership that this small group was formed with a desire to create a place where issues of sexuality and spirituality can be discussed safely. Many from the GLBT community have come through this group in an attempt to see beyond Christians and get a glimpse of God. Parents such as myself come here to gain strength and support from other parents in similar situations. Despite my wife's encouragement, I had reservations about attending my first meeting. Having taught small groups in the past, I anticipated a typical meeting format in which one person talks about his favorite subject: "Me me ME mE ME ME ME ME ME." Which is exactly what happened! I was convinced I was never going back. I was hurting. I wasn't looking for someone to "fix" my problems; I just wanted someone to care, to acknowledge my pain.

I reluctantly attended a second time. I met a guy I'll call "Arnie" who'd also found out that his son is gay. Finally, someone who communicated: "I hear your pain." Later that week, the leader of the group ("Todd") came to my house. For two hours we talked about life and how our paths had unknowingly crossed years ago. This was the first time I got off the emotional half-pipe. I was beginning to think life operated at a new normal. I always tell people you have to try a new church or group at least three times before you can write it off because it seems like whenever you "visit" some-place, you always get the guest speaker or the sermon on tithing. *(Is that all churches ever talk about?)* So I decided to take my own advice and go back to the small group a third time. This became a Defining Moment for me, and I almost missed it. It wasn't so much that I met God there, but I met God in a person whom I'll call "Don."

Don is a tall, thin man with graying hair. After living within the GLBT community for more than 30 years, he still felt an emptiness that only God could fill. The GLBT community considered him a traitor and a defector. He was physically removed from at least two churches unless he "repented of his abomination." The third church he attended, ironically, was this church. I don't know all of Don's history. And it really didn't matter at this particular moment because as I shared the events of our son's coming-out—how as a dad my heart hurt for my son and I felt like I was free-falling— this man prostrated himself on the ground (which was a little freaky for this conservative pastor) and openly wept and prayed for me and my son. For a moment, he took some of my pain and carried that burden before the Lord. *But wait… what is your position on Prop 8? Are you in a "committed relationship"? Are you a Christian? Christ-follower? Just a seeker? Are you gay, ex-gay, never gay, or ex-ex-gay?* None of that mattered. If he was willing to pray for me in ways that most of my Christian friends weren't, then this guy was my new BFF (Best Friend Forever!)

This small group has become my family...warts and all. During my time there, I've met other parents whose children (young and adult) have come out. I've met gay and lesbian people. Some say they "struggle" with homosexuality, while others have flat out said, "I struggle more with Christianity than with being gay." Finally, faces are being attached to people, and *people* are becoming the real issue—not just a proposition on a ballot.

The Job Factor

Job's healing process began when he got his focus off of himself and began praying for his friends. I'm thinking I have a lot to learn from my new friend Don. He is one of those guys I need to start praying for. On October 7, 2010, my wife and I attended our weekly small group, and I shared with Don how the day before had been a miserable day. First of all, it was an unusually rainy and cloudy day for San Diego, and I was feeling the same way on the inside. After months of riding the emotional half-pipe, enduring God's silence, feeling directionless, and lacking focus, the dam finally broke. I fell on the sofa and cried uncontrollably. After 30 minutes of falling apart, my dog Sherman climbed onto my lap. He heard my pain! He loved me unconditionally. He helped me pull it together so I could get to work and pretend that life is "fine." As I told Don this story, I noticed his countenance lift when I mentioned my dog. Don then shared a story about his childhood dog and how someday he'd like to get one of his own. I began thinking and praying about Don's situation. Less than a year before, Don had been homeless; but thanks to a few miracles, he'd just purchased a home. Since Don had been abandoned by the GLBT community and rejected by the Christian community, I was betting his new house was pretty lonely.

"Don, why don't you get a dog?"

"I'd love to get a dog, but the house cost me everything I had—and more—and it's a repo...it's a mess. The whole fence on one side is gone. I'd need to rebuild that fence before I could get a dog, and it's going to be a long time before I get the cash to do that."

"So...the only thing stopping you from getting a dog is a fence? Hmmmmm...."

The following week I showed up at Don's house with my pickup loaded with planks, posts, cement, and nails. I picked a day during the week when I thought Don might be at work. I was hoping that when he arrived home that night, he'd see all of this stuff and be pleasantly surprised. (Actually, as a high conflict-avoider, I was just trying to avoid a conflict—even a positive one.)

As fate would have it, Don had the day off and came flying out the door.

"Whoa whoa whoa whoa! What are you doing? I can't afford to reimburse you for this stuff!"

"No one asked you to. Laura asked what I wanted for my 50th birthday, and I told her I wanted to build a fence."

For the next two weeks, Don and I dug holes, poured concrete, and set fence posts. I pretended to know what I was doing, and Don pretended to help. I guess we should have measured the distance between the posts *before* we set them. Too late now! I'd just have to buy longer 2x4s. Perhaps you've heard the saying "measure twice, cut once"? Well, I'm of the mind-set that says, "Forget measuring! Keep cutting until you get it right!"

Don and I would spend an hour working on the fence and two hours talking about life, spiritual stuff, and stupid things we did in our youth. I was beginning to realize that this project had little to do with building a fence (especially one *that* crooked) and more to do with building relationships. One day, after our grueling 60 minutes of fence work, we took a break and just talked about life. I don't remember the topic, but sarcastic humor began to fly. Within minutes, Don and I were ROTFL (rolling on the floor laughing). I remember sitting up and saying: "Don, something just broke! Something popped. I wasn't faking that laugh. My heart was truly cheerful. I haven't belly laughed like that for almost a year. It feels good, like a weight has been removed. Thanks!" I think it was good for Don, too. I think Don was glad to have a friend to talk with who knew about all of his "stuff" and wasn't afraid or embarrassed to be in his company. Perhaps some day this story will be told from the other side of the fence.

"A cheerful heart is good medicine,

but a broken spirit dries up the bones."

(Proverbs 17:22 ASV)

This was an unexpected blessing that popped up somewhere along the path. (*It's not included in the price of the book, so consider this a bonus.*) Over the past year, I'm sure I've smiled. I'm sure I've even attempted to laugh—even if it was fake. But somewhere deep inside, my tank of joy had run dry. Perhaps I felt like joy would never be restored. The joy that had once been inside of me had leaked out—much like the helium in a latex balloon. The joy *tried* to rise up. But instead, it just hovered in the middle of the living room like a day-old balloon after yesterday's birthday party. It's not sinking, but it's not floating either. It's easier for it to go down than up.

That day, Don showed me that joy is not only a gift from God, but it's also a choice. Have I been "cheerful" every day since then? No. But I've recognized that it *is* possible. It isn't an on/off switch—all or nothing. It takes time, and you can't force it. But I learned to put myself in a position where joy can find me. Warning: There is laughter ahead.[66]

Journal Entry—January 27, 2011

After hours of being busy and not very productive, I'd just sat down at my desk when I received the "$1,800 phone call." [i.e., the cost of the materials for Don's fence.]

I don't know if you've looked for a puppy at "the pound," but it's part art and part science *(and part luck or faith, depending on which you believe).* If you want a pit bull, you have plenty to pick from. If you want a dog that's been abandoned because it's too old, too aggressive, or too whatever, there are plenty of those to choose from also. But if you're looking for a "cute puppy," then the pickings are slim, and there's always a waiting list of people who've signed up to adopt one. Don had already visited the pound several times, only to go home discouraged. He was particularly hopeful this week, as the pound was running a pre-Valentine's Day special—any dog for $14 (instead of the usual $70). After visiting the pound the day before, Don returned to find a three-month-old puppy that met the "cute puppy" requirement and also had no "holds" on him. *This* puppy had just found a new home!

As I picked up the phone, I could hardly filter out the excitement in his voice to hear what Don was saying: "I'm on my way home from the pound. You have to come over and see! Meet me at my house!"

After a heavy sigh of resignation that I wasn't going to get anything done today, I made the 10-minute drive. Unlatching the gate, I entered the backyard to meet "Sam." He is a German shepherd mix with beautiful markings and paws the size of polar bear mitts. This dog is going to be HUGE! Every penny spent on the fence, every muscle ache invested in digging postholes, every bruise from smacking my thumb with the hammer was suddenly dwarfed by the overflowing joy on Don's face. I guess that was my *mitzvah* (good deed) for today! *Thank you, Don, for inviting me into your life. It is an honor and a privilege.*

"He who waters will also be watered himself."

(Proverbs 11:25)

The God Whisperer

The Oasis of Great Calm

Imagine my excitement when I heard about the possibility of a *Ghostbusters III* movie coming out in 2012. "Who ya gonna call...?" Yeah, you know it! One of my favorite scenes in the first *Ghostbusters* film is when Dr. Peter Venkman (Bill Murray) turns the corner in a hotel hallway and gets hit head-on by a ghost, leaving him covered in sticky goop. "I just got slimed," he mutters from under gallons of the gooey stuff. Nothing dangerous or life-threatening. Just temporarily messy.

My first "whisper" after this season of silence wasn't so much a communication from God as it was me dumping my burden on "Greg" and walking away feeling much lighter.

(I slimed him.) My son had initially asked me not to share his coming-out with anyone. He wanted to be the one to determine who and when to communicate it to. I wanted to honor his request, but I also felt like a powder keg waiting to explode. It wasn't that I needed to *tell* someone, but I needed someone to *share this burden* with me. It was becoming too heavy for me to carry alone.

It was June of 2010, and I was a cabin counselor for a youth leadership camp in the mountains of Southern California. Each year for the past seven years, I've participated in this camp and have seen huge transformational growth in the lives of our church's youth, not to mention my own sons. Greg (a good friend of mine) was also attending the camp as a cabin counselor with his own son. Midway through the week, I just couldn't take it any longer. So I pulled Greg aside, "Got a minute?" *(He has no idea he's about to get slimed!)* We made sure our responsibilities were covered, and we pulled up a picnic table away from the crowd. I then cast all of my burdens on Greg. The watershed broke, tears flowed, and I believe Greg was speechless for the first time in his life. This was probably a good thing because Greg is one of those "fix it" personalities, and I really didn't need friends like Job's offering up their advice. I just wanted Greg to carry some of the load. That night, the first night in six months, I slept like a baby. Greg, on the other hand, was up late sharing my burden. Thank you, Greg.

Mitch Albom, in his book *Have a Little Faith*, tells the story of a man who applies for a farm job. His letters of recommendation plainly say: "He sleeps in a storm." The man is hired and sure enough, one night there is a terrible storm. While the owner of the farm is frantically running around the farm, the hired hand is sleeping soundly. As the owner checks the barn, the animals, the silos, and the bales of hay, he realizes that everything is covered, dry, and secure. And then it registers, "He sleeps in a storm."[67]

On the same day, when evening had come, He said to them, "Let us cross over to the other side." Now when they had left the multitude, they took Him along in the boat. ...And a great windstorm arose, and the waves beat into the boat, so that it was already filling. But He was in the stern, asleep on a pillow. And they awoke Him and said to Him, "Teacher, do You not care that we are perishing?"

Then He arose and rebuked the wind, and said to the sea, "Peace, be still!" And the wind ceased and there was a great calm. But He said to them, "Why are you so fearful? How *is it* that you have no faith?" And they feared exceedingly, and said to one another, "Who can this be, that even the wind and the sea obey Him!" (Mark 4:35-41)

One of my unexpected destinations along this Journey was the Oasis of Great Calm in the middle of the desert. It was a well of restoration watering a parched soul and providing for yet another day. I found that it's okay to sleep during a storm.

I Hear Your Pain

While feeling eternally stuck on the emotional half-pipe didn't help me sleep, neither did my diagnosis of sleep apnea. My wife is a Registered Nurse, and she suggested that I visit a specialist to see what could be done. So I made an appointment with Dr. Paul Coleman.[68] It seemed he had a better solution than surgery or the "iron lung" (my name for the CPAP machine) which are typical treatments for sleep apnea. After we discussed all the different options,

I was fitted for a small mouth guard and made my return appointment for three weeks out. As is typical for me, just before nodding off to sleep that first night, I offered up a quick prayer for my new doctor. This may sound strange coming from a pastor, but I really didn't expect God to *do* anything. I just meant it as a kind of an "Oh, by the way God, bless Dr. C. He seems like a nice guy." Then sometime in the middle of the night, in the middle of a dream where I'm a superhero saving the planet from evil *(too many animated movies!)*, I was shaken awake by the words, "I hear your pain." Somehow in the midst of the shock factor, I just knew that God meant Dr. Coleman. Then as I wiped the cobwebs from my eyes, I began to believe that these words would go beyond Dr. C.—perhaps even to myself and to others whom God will bring across my path.

But this is high-conflict stuff for me. What am I supposed to do with this info? Is it just to help me better pray for Dr. C.? Am I supposed to say something to him? Just as I felt the words "I hear your pain," I also sensed, "You will know what is the right thing to do." *Really!* The next morning I wrote Dr. C. a one-page letter, placed it inside a copy of the book written by Rick Warren, *The Purpose Driven Life*, and shelved it until my next appointment.

Three weeks later during my follow-up appointment, Dr. C.'s assistant helped me with my new appliance, and I could tell this thing was going to be awesome! I was holding the book (and letter) in my lap and hoping that Dr. C. would be too busy so I could just leave it on the counter as I dashed out the door. But before I could fully plan my escape, Dr. C. came into the room to explain the proper care and use of my "appliance." *I thought appliances were things like refrigerators, but whatever.* Then he asked me what book I was reading.

Suddenly, it's the moment of truth. I explained that the book was for him. And after confirming that he knows I'm a pastor, I pleaded with him not to shoot the messenger. I told him how I'd woken up in the middle of the night hearing the words "God hears your pain." I went on to say that I didn't know how his year had been, but I expected he'd had a tough one. Dr. C.'s eyes were now laser locked on mine, and I couldn't tell if he thought I was *loco in the cabeza* or if I had exposed a raw nerve that needed a root canal. Dr. C. went on to tell me about his wife who'd recently passed away, and he admitted that, yes, the last year had been extremely difficult. Somewhere between holding back the tears and being extremely professional, he gave me a firm handshake and said, "Thank you."

Even though I'm a pastor, I actually find it uncomfortable to talk to total strangers about spiritual matters. (Yes, really.) While my conversation with Dr. C. was out of my comfort zone, I've been ruminating on those words for several months now. I do believe the words are meant for me as well. Perhaps this was a Job thing where I needed to get the focus off of myself before I could begin healing. I've also shared these words with several other people whom God has brought in my path, and they, too, expressed some relief—not that the pain would be removed, but that at least their prayers are being heard and aren't just bouncing off heaven's door. (By the way, no more snoring!)

The Photo of a Thousand Questions

The Terminator revolved around the fate of Sarah Connor (Linda Hamilton) and her yet-to-be-born son, John. In a post-apocalyptic 2029, also known as the Year of Darkness, a cyborg assassin (the Terminator) is sent back to the year 1984 to kill Sarah, thereby preventing her son from becoming the future leader of the resistance. Kyle Reese (Michael Biehn), a resistance fighter, is also sent back in time to protect her and preserve the future of the resistance. Kyle is intrigued by a photograph of Sarah, which the resistance leaders gave to him to help him identify and locate the real Sarah Connor out of the hundreds listed in the phone book. In the picture, Sarah is contemplatively looking off into the distance at approaching storm clouds. There is an obvious untold story leading up to the taking of this photograph. Where was she? What was she thinking? Is her expression one of concern or hope? Why is she alone? After putting out the light in the Terminator, a pregnant Sarah goes into hiding. As she travels through Mexico, a young boy takes her picture. She buys it from him, and we then learn that it's the same photo that her son John later gave to Kyle to help track her down.

As a conflict-avoider, in the summer of 2010 I found myself quickly slipping from self-medicating to sinking into depression and then heading toward thoughts about the ultimate "out."[69] Not a good path to be on for sure! While I knew there was plenty of help available (after all, part of my job is to refer people to counseling for depression, etc.), I just didn't think there was anything humanly available that would help me. *A sure sign of depression.* Without direct divine intervention, I felt hopeless.

"Lord, I don't need to know all of the details.

But if You have a purpose in this,

if You are in the midst of this,

then I need a *picture* of hope."

I read Bible stories about people having a "vision" from God (for example, Peter and the sheet full of carnitas), and I often wonder how that works. Are they asleep? Do they go into a trance? I know it happened in biblical times and it will happen once more in the future, but is it happening *today*?[70] One morning after a restful night's sleep, I awoke with a JPEG in my mind. I recognized the people, but the event and the location didn't ring any bells. It was a simple picture with no historical memory. My son was sitting in a chair with an expression similar to that photograph in *The Terminator*, and I was sitting next to him providing comfort. What is he thinking about? What just happened? What is going to happen next? I scan the memory banks trying to find the memory that must have detached from the image. There is none to be found. This was a new image.

Journal Entry—August 26, 2010
Tonight I went to our small group meeting. (My wife stayed home to tend to our younger son.) "Joe" was

going to share his testimony with our group tonight. As a bright young college graduate, Joe had been living a double life. "Gay" at college. "Christian" at home. Tonight these two worlds would collide. His father would be there to hear about a part of Joe's life that he knew nothing about. The room was filled with more than 20 people from Joe's extended network who supported and loved *all* of Joe. Angst and nervousness almost prevented Joe from coming, but in the end, there wasn't a dry eye in the room as we all felt Joe letting go of the façade. As Joe's father leaned over to hug his son, I took a *picture* in my head. I still don't know the exact circumstances of *my* picture [of me and Seth], but this I do know: I need to be there for my son. Unconditionally. Perhaps God will use me to start a similar group at our church. A safe place to help people in their Journeys.

Borders of Concern

According to Dictionary.com, a nightmare is "a terrifying dream in which the dreamer experiences feelings of helplessness, extreme anxiety, sorrow." When I think of a nightmare, I think of another 1984 movie: *Nightmare on Elm Street*. In it a young girl has a nightmare in which objects and people begin to blur the line between dream and reality. I don't know why I let my friends drag me to see that! To this day, when I go back East to visit my family, I have to go down in the basement and check around the heater to look for that bladed glove.

On September 25, 2010, I awoke in a sweat-drenched shirt, and I was out of breath from screaming. In a state of shock, my wife tried to console me. My arm was badly cut, and in my lap was a tattered hat. *(Just kidding about that last part!)* In my dream I was being controlled much like a camera on the end of a boom. Someone else was in control of my actions causing me to turn left or right, to fly up and dart down. I was lowered into what appeared to be a giant football stadium with mile-high bleachers. The field stretched on for miles as I was carried just above ground level.

As I proceeded down the field, hundreds and hundreds of animated paintings came into view on my left and right. These paintings were similar to the ones in the dorm halls of the Harry Potter movies. As I approached each painting, the people came to life. Every one of them was a church-goer...a "Christian." Many were praying as they went about their lives. "Please don't let the rain ruin our BBQ." "Please bless this time with family." Some were praying for bigger waves, as this would be their only chance to surf that week. While I identified and connected with these people, none of them were people I recognized. Hundreds more paintings passed by me as my speed increased. Their stories, while different, each painted a similar theme. Every person had a very myopic view of their current situation. Each one was totally unaware of how their slice of sanitized Sundays was part of a grander reality that lay just beyond the border of their concerns.

Having more than my fill of paintings, the boom suddenly yanked me up and out of the stadium. As I rose above the field, I began to observe a stark contrast in the surrounding area. War. Death. Destruction. Darkness. Smoke. Nuclear explosions. In the parking lot, soldiers engaged in hand-to-hand combat. Clearly those defending the stadium were going to be overpowered. If only those *inside* the stadium would become aware and engage, this would be a completely different scenario. Ascending out of the picture, I caught the eye of a weary soldier desperately pleading for help.

The higher I went, the faster I traveled until the stadium was the size of a postage stamp. It was such a small, tranquil light in the midst of all that death and destruction. As those scenes began to roll up into one point of light or one theme, I sensed an evil presence not willing to let me escape. It wasn't a person. It wasn't a "thing." It was spiritual in nature and much bigger and more powerful than I. I felt it pulling my breath—perhaps my very soul—out of me. (Picture the

163

dementors from *Harry Potter and the Prisoner of Azkaban*.) As it stole my breath, my scream crossed over from dream to reality. As the dream lingered on, I saw my friends back in the stadium tilt their heads up as if hearing Horton for the very first time *(as in Horton Hears a Who!)*. But just before things faded to black, each went back to their lives. Things that I once felt were so important have now faded from view.

Safe Journey

During the middle weeks of October 2010, I've been repeatedly jolted awake in the middle of the night. No dreams. No pictures. Perhaps an earthquake? On the 29th at 4:15 a.m. (I'm beginning to feel like Samuel), I got up and went downstairs to read my Bible. Our church had been going through the book of Acts, and this was day four (in a row) of my being able to have a quiet time in the morning. A little bit of focus is peaking through the spiritual ADD.

In Acts chapter 27, Paul is a prisoner on a ship sailing to Rome to stand trial. In verse 10, Paul tells the crew that this voyage is going to be a disaster. Not only will the cargo and the ship be destroyed, but lives will be lost. Ignoring Paul's warning, the crew sets sail and soon encounters a very bad storm. The winds begin tossing the ship at random, and the crew tries to lighten the vessel by throwing all the tackle and equipment overboard. When all hope of survival has vanished, Paul stands to address the crew:

> "Take heart...for there stood by me this night an angel of the God to whom I belong and whom I serve, saying, 'Do not be afraid...indeed God has granted you all those who sail with you.'...I believe God that it will be just as it was told me. However, we must run aground." (Acts 27:22-26)

My Journey will lead to dry land, and we will arrive (in heaven) unharmed. But I have to let go of the rudder. I'm not capable of navigating or controlling the direction of this ship. Trust is a very difficult thing in the midst of the storm. The vessel will be destroyed, but God has granted a *Safe Journey* for all those who travel with me. It is my desire to create a space, a safe community, at our church where we can navigate the intersection of faith and sexuality in relation to self, family, and our community. Our goal is not to change one's sexuality, but rather deepen one's spirituality. My borders of concern have influenced my list of priorities down to one.

Spiritual Survival

Permit me to think out loud for a moment. Shouldn't we (me…Christians…the church) treat *all* people as children of God? If we are saved by grace through faith alone, then a person has no hope of entering the kingdom of God without belief.[71] GLBT *or* straight! On the list of priorities, **everything else** (other than faith in Christ) **is secondary**. And on my list of priorities there *is no secondary*! Not greed. Not gossip. Not alcohol abuse. Not adultery. Have I identified most, if not all, of the people "in" church? How about self-righteousness? *That should cover most of "us"!* The way I read the Bible, **Christ died for me while *I* was *still* a sinner**.[72] Whether you believe homosexuality is a sin or not is irrelevant for salvation. It's not like your personal checklist of good and bad is *all* good except for this one area. *If you'd just "fix" your sexuality, then you'd be good-to-go with God.* NO! Nothing on your (and my) checklist is good *enough* to get us into heaven. ALL have sinned and fall short of God's perfection.[73] No one does what is right according to God's standards. Our reward for missing the mark, for missing *His* standard of perfection (not the human standard of "my sin is not as bad as your sin"), is eternal separation from God.[74] One's sexuality does not separate oneself from

God any more or any less than one's self-righteous, prideful attitude. Our churches need to move from being Seeker Sensitive to Seeker Intensive. Some churches aren't even sensitive to those in our community who *want* to seek out God. There is this wall that only those on the outside can see, and it prevents people from coming in unless they first take a shower, put on a tie, or change their sexual identity.

My own church would be considered "sensitive"...a casual, come-as-you-are church. We want you to find God! I'm glad we have gays and lesbians in our church seeking God. But before I go patting myself on the back, there is still this unwritten code or wall that says, "Don't Ask, Don't Tell." You don't have to tell us, and we won't ask...that is, until you want to work in our children's ministry. Then we build the wall a little higher. We (I) need to create a place in our churches where it is safe for people to Journey toward God regardless of sexuality.

A missionary on furlough was telling his story while visiting his home church in Michigan. I haven't been able to confirm the truth of this story, nor its origin, but the application is appropriate.

While serving at a small field hospital in Africa, every two weeks I traveled by bicycle through the jungle to a nearby city for supplies.

This was a journey of two days and required camping overnight at the halfway point. On one of these journeys, I arrived in the city where I planned to collect money from a bank, purchase medicine and supplies, and then begin my two-day journey back to the field hospital. Upon arrival in the city, I observed two men fighting, one of whom had been seriously injured.

I treated him for his injuries and at the same time talked to him about the Lord Jesus Christ. I then traveled two days, camping overnight, and arrived home without incident.

Two weeks later I repeated my journey. Upon arriving in the city, I was approached by the young man I had treated. He told me that he had known I carried money and medicines. He said, "Some friends and I followed you into the jungle, knowing you would camp overnight. We planned to kill you and take your money and drugs. But just as we were about to move into your camp, we saw that you were surrounded by 26 armed guards." At this I laughed and said that I was certainly all alone in that jungle campsite.

The young man pressed the point, however, and said, "No sir, I was not the only person to see the guards. My five friends also saw them, and we all counted them. It was because of these guards that we were afraid and left you alone."

At this point in the sermon, one of the men in the Michigan congregation jumped to his feet and interrupted the missionary and asked if he could tell him the exact day this happened. The missionary told the congregation the date, and the man who'd interrupted told this story:

"On the night of your incident in Africa, it was morning here and I was preparing to go play golf. I was about to putt when I felt the urge to pray for you. In fact, the urging of the Lord was so strong, I called men in this church to meet with me here in the sanctuary to pray for you. Would all those men who met with me on that day stand up?"

The men who had met together to pray that day stood up. The missionary wasn't concerned with who they were; he was too busy counting how many men he saw. There were 26!

My prayer today is that 26 of you reading this book *(and that might be a huge assumption that 26 people will actually read this book!)* will join me in prayer and stand guard to provide a Safe Journey.

Bridge Out

As a young child, every year our family would travel to Lake Wallenpaupack (Lake Wally what? I know…) for a two-week vacation. Mom, Dad, four kids, and the dog all piled into the Oldsmobile to make the three-hour trip. We'd tow the boat packed with enough food to last us the entire trip, as there wasn't a supermarket within an hour's drive of our destination. Come to think of it, there wasn't anything within an hour's drive!

Lake Wallenpaupack is the largest man-made lake in Pennsylvania, and it's located in the Pocono Mountains. It has 52 miles of shoreline and four islands. After 14 potty breaks and 32 rounds of "Are we there yet?" we'd make the left turn and begin our descent down the tree-lined narrow road of switchbacks. Ledgedale is the hub of our little community. Not only is it the main ramp to launch your boat into the lake, but it also has (or *had*, I should say) the only phone booth within 50 miles. At the general store, you could get a loaf of bread, soft serve ice cream, Coppertone tanning *butter (long before SPF was invented)*, or the ever important *(and possibly carcinogenic)* OFF bug spray. What we really needed was the bat-be-gone spray, but that is a story for another day. Ledgedale was located at the "end" of the lake and marked the beginning of the river. I guess the actual delineation was the bridge from Ledgedale over to Indian Rocks, where we'd vacation each year.

The bridge was a post-World War II public works project made out of huge steel beams that went up, across, and down the other side. And there were a few "X" support beams in the middle that were riddled with rivets. The floor of the bridge was made out of dozens of thick wooden planks that rumbled when you drove over them. Some planks had holes in them. And not little holes either, but holes big enough for a five year old *(me)* to fall through and down into the water more than 50 feet below.

Over the years, some of the folks who lived there year-round got tired of the bridge being in such a state of disrepair. So taking matters into his own hands, someone took an acetylene torch to it and cut it down in the dark of night. *That's one sure way to move "bridge repair" to the top of the priority list!* The down side was that it added another 50-mile drive from Ledgedale down around the tip of the river and back up to Indian Rocks. I remember standing at the cliff where the bridge used to be, looking over at the ice cream stand at Ledgedale with no way to get across.

As I contemplated the thoughts of a "Safe Journey," my mind quickly went to those in the GLBT community. It seems as though they're in Ledgedale, we (Christians) are in Indian Rocks, and the bridge is out. I'm not sure if the Christians or the GLBT community cut down the bridge. But in the midst of ruminating on my bridge analogy and thinking I was on to something new, I began reading the book *Love Is an Orientation* by Andrew Marin. Not only did he already have the bridge analogy, but he used the Golden

Gate Bridge, which is definitely more recognizable than the Lake Wallenpaupack Bridge.[75]

The point is, God has whispered to both of us (and probably others) with a very similar word picture. The Christian community is on one side; the GLBT community is on the other side—and the bridge is out. In my vision, my son is swimming somewhere in the middle and being forced to decide which shore to swim to. Even though he isn't drowning (yet), I dive in after him and soon realize it will take more than just me to rescue him. As I look back at the Christian shoreline, I begin to see *my world* from a different perspective. Thinking that others will surely come into the water to help me, I see most people going about their business as usual—seemingly unaware that we're floundering—and feeling unconcerned about the need for a bridge.

I've been devouring all kinds of books on the issue of sexuality and the church. Books written by moms who've navigated this issue. Books from parachurch ministries explaining how people become gay most often because of environmental factors, including an absent or abusive father. I'm not convinced environment is *the* factor, but I'm open to the fact that it may be *a* factor. What I found lacking were books written from the dad's perspective. Where are the dads who, even though they may not understand this issue, aren't willing to abandon their children because of it?

I also found some books written by pastors, and I was shocked. If this is what the GLBT community sees when it looks across the water toward the Christian community, then it's no wonder they are not interested. I found a lot of pastors quoting Leviticus and translating key words from the original language. I didn't see a whole lot of John 3:16. I didn't see a whole lot of "Love thy neighbor" but lots of "Who *is* my neighbor?" There was one book in particular that had a couple of eye-opening points that I would love to quote. But to be honest, I'm embarrassed to cite the source. However, I'll try my best to write what was communicated to me through this particular book:

> *(Spoken in the most snooty, looking-down-my-nose voice possible)* We, the highly educated, appointed by God, and confirmed by others who are even more highly educated than we are, are here to impart wisdom from above to you the struggling sinner. Once you've been enlightened with the truth of the intended meaning from the original language of the Scriptures, the only possible conclusion will be for

you to repent. It's a spiritual word we use for what's more commonly referred to as "turn or burn." Hence, we shall offer you the right hand of fellowship—with just a few conditions, of course!

Stunned, I fell back in my chair and several thoughts came to mind. My first thought was that I'd better not write down my first thought. If I did, I'd have to filter out the verbs I'd use to tell the author what he can do with this book. *I'm sure the verbs I'd use would be self-explanatory without requiring parsing from the original language.*

My second thought was to recognize that I'm floundering between two shorelines and I need some help. Perhaps I should give the writer the benefit of the doubt and try to identify his intended audience. Surely it must be "pastor types". He can't possibly think someone from the GLBT community is actually going to pick up this book. But written in the pages it clearly states that the hope of this book was to offer encouragement to the person(s) who struggles with this "sin." *Really!* I'm not exactly Mr. Wizard here, but I'll go out on a limb and suggest that *maybe* this isn't a bestseller in the Rainbow Bookstore. What I thought would be a life preserver of grace turned out to be a shipwreck of law.

Another thought I had was that this author obviously doesn't have a horse in this race. This was just an intellectual exercise for him. I don't think he truly wrestled with God on this issue. If he did, I'd like to see his limp. I find it difficult to trust pastors who don't limp, who aren't vulnerable with their own issues.[76]

Why does the Christian community offer unconditional grace to every other "sin" except this one? Churches invest a lot of resources to go to Haiti, Uganda, Turkmenistan, and the remotest places on earth with the message of unconditional love. I'm not saying we shouldn't do that—we should. Yet at the same time, we're unwilling to build a bridge to the other side of town. Forget for a moment the other side of town—what about the people in our own congregations? We have people who are living as though they are in *The Diving Bell* desperately seeking to be released as *the Butterfly*.[77] They are screaming on the inside for someone to point them toward God, but no one hears them. If you *struggle* with alcohol, we have a place for you. If you *struggle* with same-sex attraction, there IS a place for you...but it's not here! And don't even *think* about working in our children's ministry! No wonder most in the GLBT community *struggle* with Christianity more than they struggle with their sexuality.

When building a bridge (especially if it's a long-span one), a foundation is placed in the middle of it. In the case of the Golden Gate Bridge, there are actually *two* huge foundations. One is closer to the northern shoreline, while the second foundation is closer to the southern shoreline. I believe one of my roles going forward in this Journey is to build a foundation just off the "Christian" shoreline. And then I think I'll hold up my sign to the GLBT community. All it will say is:

GOD HEARS YOUR PAIN.

I believe there are many within the GLBT community who'd be interested in knowing their Creator if we could just get some of the Christians out of the way. My hope is that someone might see my sign or perhaps notice my limp and be willing to build a foundation just off the GLBT shoreline. My goal isn't necessarily to build a bridge between the two shorelines. Maybe someday that will happen. But for today, my only desire is to maybe lift a few people out of the water long enough to catch their breath. Instead of looking to swim to either shoreline, they should be able to stop treading water long enough to look up into the eyes of a God who desperately loves them. A God who loves them enough to hit people like me with a meteor—not intending to destroy me, but rather to alter my course. *To break my heart for what breaks His.* And what breaks His heart is that there are a lot of people in a lot of different communities who'd love to know their Creator, but they just can't see Him beyond the people who claim to represent Him.

Time is short and this season we call "life" will end soon. When the game is over and all the pieces go back in the box, we realize that the game, the board, and all of the pieces belong to God.[78] The things we're so concerned about today will soon be swallowed up in eternity, and then only one thing will matter. You may want to start getting to know the One who holds all the pieces.

The LORD is *near* to those who have a broken heart,
And saves such as have a contrite spirit. (Psalm 34:18)

Shadow Destinations

O ne thing I noticed as I began wandering in the desert was the attractiveness of some shadow destinations that appeared in the form of some pretty tempting mirages. Most of them had something to do with seeking comfort and avoiding pain. In the words of the great theologian James T. Kirk (William Shatner), *Star Trek*'s commander of the *U.S.S. Enterprise*, "My pain has made me who I am."

I have learned that pain is a much more efficient tool than comfort at helping me better align my life with God's plan. By taking the shadow destination called "Quick and Easy," I may miss some of the Defining Moments that God has prepared for me in the desert. And by missing some of those Defining Moments, I place myself in the position of being ill equipped and unprepared for the next phase of my Journey on the other side of the desert.

Remember the Israelites in the desert? Yes, God was going to give them the Promised Land. But entering the city of Jericho (and other cities along the way) would require obedience toward God. It was a teachable moment that was repeated in the desert until they got it right. *I would much rather learn it right the first time than spend 40 years in the desert trying to avoid it.*

Several months ago I was teaching the third through fifth grade kids at our church, and I was trying to get across the concept of Jesus being the "light of the world."[79] I started with the question "Does darkness exist?" Most of the kids talked about how their bedrooms got dark after their parents turned out the light at night, and so the conclusion was "Yes, darkness exists." So wearing my scientific lab coat, my magnifying glass and a prop labeled DARKNESS O METER in my hand, I set out to measure darkness. As I asked the kids for their help, I fielded possible solutions that sounded good but still left me unable to measure darkness. My conclusion: If it cannot be measured scientifically, then darkness does not exist!

I then asked if light existed and how it could be measured. I pulled out my light meter and was able to show them how the meter moved based on the amount of light it detected. I asked the kids, "What is the source of light?" I got the obvious answers of light bulb, flashlight, and the sun. I pulled out my flashlight and showed them the bulb and the batteries. While they are necessary to *have* light, the source of the light was actually *me*! I was the one who turned on and off the light *(and shined it in their eyes, of course)*. "What is the *source* of light for the sun?" Hydrogen...fire.... "Yes, those are important to *have* light, but *who* is the source?" The answer to almost every question in kid's church is either "Jesus" or "God." And so we talked about God being the source of all light and that darkness was really the absence of light (God). We talked about eternity with God (light) and eternity without God (darkness). I cannot imagine spending eternity without God and without light.

It's hard to explain to someone what it's like to walk in the comfort and warmth of God's light if they've never experienced it. Explaining what it's like to have fellowship with the Creator of the universe to someone who's never experienced it is virtually impossible. I admire Mother Teresa for reaching out and meeting the physical and spiritual needs of people who've never known what it's like to have fellowship with their Creator. Mother Teresa confessed that without her "interior darkness," she would not have known the longing for love (light) and the pain of feeling unloved (darkness). In a sense, God said, "I hear your pain, poorest of the poor in India," and He broke Mother Teresa's heart for what breaks His—in this case, a group of people living with the label "unlovable" who'd been cast out by society. As painful as it was, Mother Teresa came to accept her "interior darkness" as a necessary part of God's work in her life. Perfect light casts out darkness...including the shadows.

"For the first time in this eleven years—I have come to love the darkness—for I believe now that it is a part, a very, very small part of Jesus' darkness and pain on earth. You have taught me to accept it [as] a 'spiritual side' of 'your work.'"[80]

Life in an Open Cadence

The 1988 Disney film *Who Framed Roger Rabbit* offers a good example of the frustration that an open cadence can cause. The storyline revolves around a real-life detective (Bob Hoskins) who's investigating a murder involving the cartoon character of Roger Rabbit (voiced by Charles Fleischer). In one scene the detective tries to entice Roger out of hiding by going around the room and tapping part of the classic seven-note cadence: "Shave and a haircut..." on the walls. Each time, the cartoon character is shown in his hiding spot behind the wall, trying desperately not to finish the phrase. Finally, Roger Rabbit is unable to restrain himself. He's compelled to finish the phrase and bring the cadence to resolution—ultimately giving away his hiding place.

In music theory *cadence* is a progression or pattern of chords that indicates a section of the music is concluding. Cadence is to music what certain marks of punctuation are to the written word, such as a pause (comma), finality (period), or dramatic closure (exclamation point). While it's difficult to give musical examples in writing, most people recognize "Shave and a haircut..." The authentic or "perfect" cadence would be to conclude with "two bits!" It not only signals the end of a phrase, but it's also "the end." The listener knows nothing more is coming. "Shave and a haircut..." by itself represents what's known as a half or "open" cadence. It's unresolved, suspended, incomplete, and downright annoying! Sometimes directors intentionally leave you hanging during a movie, as was the case of the spinning top at the end of the 2010 film *Inception*. The cadence of the movie was resolved with a *deceptive* cadence or "comma," not an "exclamation point" so as to leave the viewer content with the end of the story, yet still desiring a sequel.

In real life, things don't always resolve themselves as they do in a 30-minute sitcom or within the time frame of a movie. This can cause tension, anxiety, and even frustration. This explains why by the time we got to *Rocky IV,* we were done! There needs to be finality and closure. The movie needs to come to an authentic end or perfect cadence.

Perhaps it's my Golden Retriever personality (faithful companion), but I don't like having open cadences in my life. I find myself lying awake at night trying to bring res-olution to all of life's problems. If you've listened to the news lately, some of the world's issues are daunting and can become paralyzing. Even if I focus only on the issues in my personal life, there are still too many plates to keep spin-ning, and sooner or later they'll come crashing down.[81] In an effort to simplify life, I bring to conclusion the plates of lesser importance as quickly and easily as I can, and then I put them neatly on the shelf (resolved at least temporarily).

As I mentioned earlier, women in ministry was not a life-or-death issue to me when I was a young pastor. But that changed when it became an issue at our church. Apart from the differing viewpoints, the number of people who were unwilling to "un-resolve" this issue and give that plate another spin surprised me.[82] There seemed to be a stubborn-ness, a resistance, an "unteachable" spirit that made it impos-sible to find common ground. Having a disagreement over an issue can be unnerving for my personality type, but when people depart the church and leave the issue unresolved, that also leaves me with an open cadence in life. Now the issue for me is no longer women in ministry, but a broken relationship that's demanding resolution. In an effort to try and bring an internal resolve, I'm forced to place it back on the shelf labeled "Grace." Depending on the number of plates one already has spinning in life, I guess bringing back one more plate that was already resolved is easier said than done.

As I read and study the Bible, it's clear to me that the apex of the story is wrapped up in the life, death, and resurrection of Jesus Christ. The most important open cadence in life is the relationship between Creator and creation. The completed work on the cross invites us to evaluate the universal dissonance in our lives that begs for an authentic cadence. Every other aspect of life—whether or not it's mentioned in the Bible—pales in comparison to this one issue. My life story will come to resolution—an authentic cadence—based solely on the one issue of "How do I resolve the dissonance in my life against the backdrop of the cross?"

As I take the issue of sexuality back off the shelf and un-resolve it, I do so with the understanding that while I might be able to go further down the path of understanding, ultimately I'm not going to be able to resolve every point of contention within this issue—especially in the time frame of my life, much less during the writing of this book.

In this chapter I'd like to identify and briefly comment on some issues that I am forced to put back on the shelf to be resolved at a later date. There is no <Pause> button on life that will let me take the time to examine each issue to its end today. Even if I had the time, there are some issues that may not be resolved this side of heaven. The tension comes into play in that "how I do life" tomorrow (as a pastor and a father) is dependent upon, to some extent, how, when, and if I resolve part or all of this issue.

The items listed below will be developed further—perhaps as part of another book—another day. However, today I must be content to identify these issues and wait for God to add His "two bits."

Inborn vs. Environmental

Everyone has a bias, so let me just state my biases up front. My first bias is toward ignorance. I don't know enough about this subject, and I'm finding there are plenty of books and scientific studies out there that I could spend a lifetime researching and still come to the same conclusion that is currently my second bias: That the cause of homosexuality is probably a combination of both genetics and environment. There is something a person is born with that predisposes him or her toward one form of sexuality over another. My tension with this issue lies in the assumption that if it's "inborn," then it's natural and therefore should be accepted as "good"; and if it's environmental, then somehow we have the ability to change a "bad" situation into a "good" one.

There are many things that are attributable to genetics. Some are considered good and desirable. That's why people pay millions of dollars to breed a winning thoroughbred hoping to pass on the positive genes. There are other attributes that while they're acceptable, they're not necessarily good. I'm told I can blame my baldness on my mother's father. If so, then my kids are doomed to be bald! While baldness may not be desirable, I'm really not all that motivated to "correct" it. There are other conditions attributable to genetics such as Downs Syndrome and cleft palate that we'd put in the category of undesirable *and* unacceptable. Conditions such as cancer and ADHD both seem to ascribe to a source that is a combination of genetics and environment. While I think this is an interesting issue that's worthy of more research, the end-all conclusion has little impact on my spiritual foundation. And that foundation is a Creator-God who is perfect and a creation that is imperfect and, as the second law of thermodynamics states, in a constant state of decay, both genetically and environmentally.

As an aside: I am awestruck by the number of people who think the world would be a better place if we all just sold our SUVs and bought electric vehicles. Really? Personally, I think that if everyone on the planet sold their SUVs and bought electric vehicles, the problem of having to dispose of all those electric batteries would considerably outweigh the "damage" SUVs are currently causing the environment. Also, how many SUVs would we have to get rid of in order to offset one burst from Mount Pinatubo or Mount St. Helens? What's the impact on ocean temperature from any one of the numerous underwater volcanoes spewing noxious fumes and molten lava into the ocean on a daily basis? My guess is even if we removed all of the vehicles from the planet, we'd still be in trouble. How's that for a slightly less-than-convenient truth!

In a sense our global climate condition is both environmental *and* genetic. There are some things we can do to "change" our condition. But whether or not we change, ultimately there is still a bigger issue that needs to be addressed: We live in a fallen world that is in desperate need of a Savior.

Back to our discussion on inborn versus environmental...

I talked to a few gay teens recently, and I examined their "research" that they claimed "proves" homosexuality is 99.99 percent genetic, that it's "all in the genes," and therefore part of God's original plan of creation. I'm curious how an 18 year old has managed to find such evidence that still eludes me in my own research. One young man pointed me to a scientific research report that he was using for proof and the foundation on which he was about to build his future life decisions.[83] While I shared his optimism, I don't think he shared my skepticism.

I mentioned my biases earlier, but regardless of my beliefs, I'm intrigued that someone has found "proof" to incorporate into one's personal core values and beliefs. This young man gladly gave me the Web site link to the report. I believe "Trust but verify" was the motto of the early Bereans in the Bible. So I went to the Web site in hopes of actually reading the report. I saw the promo blurb indicating a possible genetic link to a person's sexuality. It was worded in such a way as to be ambiguous, yet it was revealing enough to entice you to want to purchase the full report. I clicked on the report and was immediately prompted to enter my credit card information. (Here was my first clue that this young man had probably stopped reading at the blurb.) *Fifty dollars! Are you serious?* Now I *know* he didn't read the full report! After pausing a few moments to determine whether or not I can write this off as a business expense, I purchased the report. Then I spent several hours trying to read and understand the "doctor speak" in it. I'm grateful for Dictionary.com and other medical terminology Web sites for explaining some words that I couldn't use in a complete sentence if my life depended upon it. Although I am educated far beyond my intelligence, I did find a few words and sentences I understood.

"Evidence is riddled with *inconsistencies.*"

"Two further studies *failed* to replicate these patterns, finding instead that homosexual males did *not* differ significantly from heterosexual males…"

"Found *no evidence* of this, contradicting the theory."

"Larger samples are needed to confirm that real effects exist, *if* indeed they do."

"Reported *no* sex differences and *no association* between gender identity or sexual orientation and dermatoglyphic pattern."

"*Lacks* any direct quantitative evidence..."[84]

I appreciate this young man's desire to bring this issue to a perfect cadence. For him, his conclusions and decisions will significantly impact the path of his life. I don't need a PhD to understand that this report was not the "proof" upon which to build any foundation. My heart goes out to young people who are trying to bring an understanding of how their sexuality and theology interact. To make matters worse, when these young people come to the church, they are met either with an awkward unwillingness to dialogue on the subject or worse—they're given the right boot of fellowship right out the back door. As much as I dislike an open cadence, closing your eyes and stopping your ears does not make the issue resolve itself.

Ex-Gay vs. No Way

There are several parachurch ministries out there that claim they've helped many people become "ex-gay" and go on to live a heterosexual life. I've read the stories and met and talked with people who've left the gay lifestyle, which seems to indicate that "change" is possible. First Corinthians 6:9-11 also seems to indicate that people with a whole bunch of different issues have been able to change.[85] Yet there are just as many testimonies of people who've tried to change, desired to change, sought out change, and still were unable to change. So the cadence of "Can a person change?" remains open.

Andrew Marin, in his book *Love Is an Orientation*, states that only about 20 percent of GLBT people seek to "change" their orientation.[86] That means 80 percent are content in saying "no thanks!" "While most homosexuals will admit change is possible, most just don't feel the need to do so."[87] Of the 20 percent who seek out "change," most parachurch ministries report approximately a 67 percent success rate.[88] So in a best-case scenario, out of 100 people only 15 actually report some form of "change." That leaves 85 people either with no desire for change or the belief that trying to change was a failure or a mistake.

As I pondered the open cadence of "change," echoing in my ear was the familiar question: *What difference does it make? Is "change" the goal?* If we found the Minoxidil for human sexuality and everyone was "cured," would that change anything? No! We'd still live in a broken world— only now everybody would be broken heterosexuals in need of a perfect God. Sexuality is a horizontal issue. Holiness is a vertical issue. Regardless of whether or not a person can change, as a pastor, my job is to help people draw closer to God, to "be holy, for I am holy."[89] "The opposite of homosexuality is not heterosexuality—it's holiness."[90]

Marriage vs. Union

I remember several years ago when Christians were encouraged to boycott certain stores because of their contributions to pro-gay political activities. As recently as February 4, 2011, CNN Belief Blog Co-Editor Dan Gilgoff reported on the problems that Chick-fil-A was allegedly having over its contribution to "pro-marriage" political activities.[91] Once again I find myself perplexed as to why this is such a dividing issue. In putting out my biases first, I personally subscribe to the union as described in the Bible: One man and one woman before God. As a pastor I up hold that union before God. Whether or not the state of California or the federal government recognizes that union is irrelevant to me. I didn't get married in hopes of obtaining a tax break or any particular legal status. I don't perform marriages so people will have any particular economic advantage. In the true sense of Separation of Church and State, I'd prefer the state (government) stay out of the affairs of the church. If the goal of Proposition 8 was to equalize benefits for gay unions and heterosexual marriages, then remove any extra (governmental) benefits currently extended to marriages. As a Christ-follower, I don't look to the state or any other organization to validate or invalidate how I practice my faith.

However, I also find it rather perplexing to see how much effort the GLBT community is expending to demand affirmation from faith-based groups for their identity or their unions. The single group that the GLBT community is most at odds with is the very group they now seek validation from. The way our (California) government is set up, if enough people vote for and pass a proposition that would legalize gay unions, then the state of California would be legally bound to recognize them. First of all, if the will of the people voted for gay unions, then regardless of my beliefs it's now become a law and I respect that. It still doesn't change my faith-based practices in marriage. I don't have a problem with the state recognizing or not recognizing any union or organization as long as it's voted on in the appropriate manner. Again, I think it's odd that the church is taking such a firm stand on Proposition 8 to "defend" marriage. If they were successful in making gay unions forever illegal, would that change anything?

If a bill were introduced *legalizing* same-sex marriages throughout the United States and it was forever unchange-able, or if a bill were introduced *banning* same-sex marriages and could never be repealed, which would you want? My point is, neither one matters! It's already out there—65,000 adopted children live with gay parents; 14,000 foster chil-dren live in gay or lesbian homes.[92] Legalizing or banning it is not going to make it go away. Christians have ignored the elephant in the room hoping not to have this conversation with their kids. But it's there! Our kids are already going to school with little Johnny who has two moms. Preventing the school library from putting certain books in the schools isn't going to stop us from having to have this difficult conversation.

The church adopted "Don't Ask, Don't Tell" long before President Clinton made it a policy. The church has been willing to ignore the obvious but difficult discussion that really needs to take place. The issue is not about making gay unions legal or illegal. The fact is they exist whether or not you want to recognize them. The issue is not whether sexuality is inborn or environmental. The issue is not keeping Christians out of politics or politics out of Christians. The issue is not to say that my church or your church is "sensitive" toward gays and lesbians…as long as they "don't tell." The issue is that God is seeking the GLBT community to bring them to Himself. As difficult as this discussion is, I don't want to be blocking anyone's view of God. So for now, I have to temporarily resolve these open cadences as best I can by leaving them to be revisited later. So I pause, slightly more educated and significantly more aware of those around me. God hears your pain, and He desperately wants you to experience Him.

Atypical

While some may use the term *typical* to mean "normal" or "average," I use it here more along the lines of an emblem or a symbolic representative of a larger group. As a culture we want to quickly label people groups so we can decide who we'll associate with — without actually having to get to know anybody within that group. We label the Northeast as "uptight," the Southeast as the "Bible belt," the Midwest as "hicks," and the West as "surfer dudes." Born in Philadelphia and having lived in San Diego for more than 20 years, I don't think I fit either label that one might try to affix on me.

My *typical* view of a gay man has been that of a person who's grown up without a father, been abused as a child, and made poor choices leading him into a life of reckless sexual abandonment. Needless to say, my old label has now been significantly challenged. According to some research, less than 15 percent of the GLBT community was abused as a child.[93] While I'm not the perfect father, it's easily verifiable that I'm not absent from my sons' lives, nor am I abusive. Keeping my label in place has afforded me the opportunity of *not* having to address this issue for many years. But now that it's hit home, my label has been torn off, and I'm seeing individual names and faces—some for the first time. My typical label of an entire people group has become atypical.

In talking with my son, I realize another atypical part of this situation is that this isn't something he chose. Seth did not wake up one day and *decide* to be attracted to members of the same gender any more than I chose to be attracted to my wife. (When I saw her at the Philly train station, it was more like that scene in *Bambi* where Thumper meets the girl rabbit and "Boing!") I did, however, make a decision to be a Christ-follower (as did my son). Because of my decision, I've taken on the identity or label of "Christian." Viewing that label as best I can through the eyes of the GLBT community, I am seeing a not-so-accurate, yet *typical* label for the larger "Christian" group. Nonetheless, my identity is with Christ. I don't feel it's necessary to hyphenate my identity with other labels to further describe me as a person. While "balding-white-middle-aged-conservative-*slightly*-overweight-American-heterosexual Christian" might be more accurate, I find "Christian" to be sufficient because it recognizes my *chosen* identity, rather than the things I have no control over. So I have to admit that I struggle with the label "Gay Christian." Is that a choice? We don't say "Heterosexual Christian." Should we say "Alcoholic Christian" or "Left-Handed Christian"? I'm afraid I have another open cadence! What I'm beginning to understand is that what appears to be typical is not representative of the larger of either group. What I thought to be atypical (our situation) is much more commonplace than I expected.

While the GLBT community has largely labeled Christians as judgmental, what is the typical label(s) the church gives itself in relation to this issue of sexuality? Kerby Anderson, in his book *A Biblical View of Homosexuality*, describes five typical churches:

1. **The Permissive Church.** It's heavy on compassion, light on biblical teaching on the subject. *"We don't want to offend anyone, so we don't talk about it."*

2. **The Rebellious Church.** Its openly gay membership celebrates all manner of sexuality without regard to biblical teaching. *"Sure it was an abomination then, but not now. It's no different than eating shrimp."*

3. **The Judgmental Church.** It's all judgment and no compassion. *"Jesus hates fags."*

4. **The Uncommitted Church.** It withholds judgment and compassion, yet provides no help to the GLBT community. *"This is such a divisive issue. I'm not sure what to do."*

5. **The Ignorant Church.** Not really sure what the Bible teaches on this subject, it provides no help to the people involved in this issue. *"We'll keep praying. The Lord knows!"*[94]

Once again I find myself uncomfortable with the typical labels. My desire is for my church to be atypical, living in that open cadence between theology and compassion, between judgment and grace.

> "You therefore, my son, be strong in the *grace*
> that is in Christ Jesus."
> (2 Timothy 2:1, *emphasis added*)

As John Ortberg writes in his book *Faith and Doubt*: "There are certain votes from which it is impossible to abstain, what William James called *forced* decisions. For example, if you decide to put off making a decision about getting in shape, your body will decide for you."[95] Ignoring Scripture regardless of my interpretation is not an option. Conveniently redefining Scripture to provide for my current circumstances is not an option. Standing firm on the literal interpretation of *all* the Scriptures (God said it, I believe it, that settles it!) would suggest that I take my son out back and stone him to death! Most Christians, even those who are literal in their interpretation, would say we don't do that anymore.

My son, gay or not, loves the Lord more than a significant number of people sitting in a *typical* church service do. If we literally interpret *all* of the verses in the Bible, than there are lots of other issues mentioned as "abominations" before the Lord that the church may need to reexamine and un-resolve. My belief is that if we killed by stoning everyone who commits an *abomination* before the Lord, then churches all across America would be empty the following week! You who are without sin cast the first stone![96]

I will save my discussion on interpreting Scripture for the next chapter. For now, I'm trying to identify where I as a father and a pastor should go from here. Once again I find the path to be atypical in trying to maintain a healthy tension of theology and compassion that will produce positive growth in my family and in my church. I desire to pursue truth regardless of my own or anyone else's interpretation of Scripture. I desperately need grace; and from what I'm seeing with regard to this issue, that grace is being hoarded within the walls of Christiandom.

Clint McCance is a member of the Arkansas school board, and he was recently quoted in *The Huffington Post*.[97] He was responding to a popular Facebook initiative asking people to show their support for gay youths in response to a recent wave of suicides.

Seriously they want me to wear purple because five queers killed themselves. The only way im wearin it for them is if they all commit suicide. I cant believe the people of this world have gotten this stupid. We are honoring the fact that they sinned and killed themselves because of their sin. REALLY PEOPLE. [sic]

McCance's response to one detractor asking him to reconsider his words:

No because being a fag doesn't give you the right to ruin the rest of our lives. If you get easily offended by being called a fag, then dont tell anyone you are a fag. Keep that s*** to yourself. I dont care how people decide to live their lives. They dont bother me if they keep it to thereselves. It pisses me off though that we make a special purple fag day for them. I like that fags cant procreate. I also enjoy the fact that they often give each other aids and die. If you arent against it, you might as well be for it. [sic]

After one commenter invoked McCance's Christianity and his willingness to seemingly talk hatefully about the families of other people, McCance responded with:

I would disown my kids [if] they were gay. They will not be welcome at my home or in my vicinity. I will absolutely run them off. Of course my kids will know better. My kids will have solid christian beliefs. See it infects everyone. [sic]

"We have met the enemy and he is us."[98] Here is reason number two for my wanting to jump off the "Christian" ramp in my bridge analogy! I am dumbfounded by such hate and ignorance coming from someone claiming to be saved by grace. REALLY PEOPLE! Please don't give this man a rock and keep him away from my son because he just might use it!

"Judge not, that you be not judged. For with what judgment you judge, you will be judged, and with the measure you use, it will be measured back to you. And why do you look at the speck in your brother's eye, but do not consider the plank in your own eye? Or how can you say to your brother, 'Let me remove the speck from your eye'; and look, a plank *is* in your own eye? Hypocrite! First remove the plank from your own eye, and then you will see clearly to remove the speck out of your brother's eye." (Matthew 7:1-5)

"And though I have the gift of prophecy, and understand all mysteries and all knowledge, and though I have all faith, so that I could remove mountains, but have not love, I am nothing." (1 Corinthians 13:2)

"A life without love is worthless." — Rick Warren[99]

In Matthew 22:36, Jesus was asked the question: "Teacher, which is the greatest commandment in the law?" He responded with something close to, "Love God with everything you have, and love your neighbor as yourself" (my paraphrase of Matthew 22:37).

I have respected your freedom of speech, Mr. McCance. Now respect mine:

Both of my sons have "solid Christian beliefs." I see my son sharing his faith (drawing people to Christ instead of repelling them) with kids who've been kicked out of churches similar to the one you probably attend. These are kids who desperately want to know God, but their view of God is blocked by people like you who claim to represent God. Young kids who are wrestling with something they didn't ask for. They are reaching out to parents, youth pastors, and people they should be able to trust to help them understand why they feel different than others. They are taught in Sunday school and churches about a God who loves them unconditionally. God can forgive your abuse of alcohol. God can forgive your adultery, greed, slander, and gossip. Yet this one "sin" our culture has elevated above all else as the unpardonable sin. Even if one interprets the Bible to say homosexuality is a sin, it really isn't talked about all that much in the Bible. The Bible has far more verses dedicated to the love of money and self-righteous pride. Will you disown your kids if they become greedy or prideful? Will you run them off for being slanderers? Of course not! Your kids will "know better." Maybe you should read the latter part of Romans chapter 7:

"For we know that the law is spiritual, but I am carnal, sold under sin. For what I am doing, I do not understand, for what I will to do, that I do not practice; but what I hate, that I do...I know that in me (that is, in my flesh) nothing good dwells...for I delight in the law of God according to the inward man. But I see another law in my members, warring against the law of my mind, and bringing me into captivity to the law of sin which is in my members. O wretched man that I am! Who will deliver me from this body of death?...There is therefore now **no condemnation** to those who are in Christ Jesus." (Romans 7:14–8:1, *boldfaced emphasis added*)

It is not a question about knowing the law. I know what the law says. The bar is set pretty high. Jesus *raised* the bar even further out of reach by saying that if you even *look* at another woman with lust, you've already committed adultery with her in your heart.[100]

"For whoever shall keep the whole law,
and yet stumble in one point, he is guilty of all."
(James 2:10)

Are you trying to tell me you've never had a sinful thought?

"For all *(including you, me, the heterosexual community, and the GLBT community)* have sinned *(stumbled on at least one point, whether in attitude, finances, sexuality, or even just thought life)* and fall short of the glory of God." (Romans 3:23)

As a father and a pastor, I find your words troubling and contradictory to the "Good News" you allegedly subscribe to. While your words may not be infectious, they are definitely cancerous. If you're easily offended by being called an a**hole, then don't tell anyone you're an a**hole. Keep that s*** to yourself. (Note to Self: *Ease up on the caffeine! I am wired!*)

Unfortunately, yours is the stuff that gets printed as the *typical* Christian message. I will continue to try and follow Christ's words to "love God" and "love others" above all else, which includes working out my theology on other issues such as divorce, women in ministry, pride, the use of alcohol, greed, drums in church, sexuality, and my recent relapse into the use of foul language. I choose to distance myself from the typical.

SHIFT

"Sometimes we need increased momentum in our lives. We feel like something is a little off, we are lugging a little too slow or somehow we need a surge of "juice." That's when it's time for a SHIFT. This isn't about going in the wrong direction. This isn't a U-turn. It's about executing a gear change, it's about an adjustment that will give us momentum. A SHIFT....We only have so much energy, so let's use it wisely, let's make sure we're in the right gear, let's SHIFT!" —Ed Noble, Senior Pastor at Journey Community Church[101]

From 1983 to 1986, one of my favorite TV shows was NBC's *The A-Team*. The A-Team was a group of U.S.

Army Special Forces personnel who where branded as war criminals for crimes they didn't commit. While on the run, they always found themselves in a situation in which they'd have to risk exposing their true identities while doing good and helping the oppressed. Throughout the entire show, there was always a sense that *These guys have no idea what they're doing!* Yet by the end of the hour, the audience could see there'd been a master plan in place all along. Currently, I'm not quite sure how things are going to work out in my own situation, but I'm trusting that there's a Master Plan. I just wish I knew what it was!

As I stumble through life and try to stay on the path that I believe God desires me to follow, there are times when I get off course and a necessary (usually painful) adjustment is required. At other times, though, I seem to stumble in the right direction, which is then confirmed by other people or situations that are beyond my control thereby giving the appearance of a master plan (not unlike The A-Team). This is one of those situations. As I wrap up my season in the desert, my season of testing and trial, my internal darkness, I'm beginning to shift my thoughts to the future: *Okay, where do I go from here? What have I learned? What changes do I need to make in order to prepare for what the Lord has in store for me?* So I quickly jotted down several things that I've learned. Most of them don't require a complete U-turn, but I do need to make a shift.

For most of the last seven years, my relationship with God has been cruising along in fifth gear. The path of life was a wide-open road, and I could cover a lot of distance without having to expend too much energy. But this past year has brought my spiritual life back down to second gear, which put a lot of stress on the engine. Cruising on the freeway of life was no longer an option. Second gear is fine for meandering through my neighborhood. But at some point I'll need to *up*shift to third gear in order to gain the proper momentum to re-engage in traffic and eventually attempt driving on the freeways of Southern California again. I'm sensing my walk with the Lord is about to upshift into third gear. The sound of the engine indicates the approaching need for a gear change.

While driving as a teenager, I'd often make second gear scream and then skip third gear altogether and go right into the cruise mode of fourth gear. While I'm now tempted to skip third gear and go right back to cruising the freeways, I'm also sensing this next season of life is meant to be spent in third gear. This season will be a time of continued preparation and increasing momentum. As I was pondering the list of possible life-shifts coming my way, I attended a church leadership meeting and heard our senior pastor, Ed Noble, announce the title of his next sermon series: SHIFT. Ed then laid out the five *shifts* that he believed our congregation needed to make in the coming months. I smiled! Inside I was thinking, *I love it when a plan comes together!*

With the A-Team's adventures, there always seemed to be a little "luck" involved. I don't see any luck here, but a God-orchestrated plan coming together. My initial shift—and probably the most important one—came out of the series of messages that our church had just finished.

The Jesus Creed[102]

"Jesus answered him, 'The first of all the commandments is: *"Hear, O Israel, the LORD our God, the LORD is one. And you shall love the LORD your God with all your heart, with all your soul, with all your mind, and with all your strength."* This *is* the first commandment. And the second, like *it*, is this: *"You shall love your neighbor as yourself."* There is no other commandment greater than these.'" (Mark 12:29-31)

At least once a year, our church does a series in which *everyone* reads through and studies the same material. From the children's ministry on up through the middle school and high school, plus all of our home groups, recovery ministries, and care groups are on the same page with what's being taught on Sunday mornings. There's something transformational about downshifting and spending several weeks navigating the same portion of Scripture, rather than just cruising over it in one weekend service.

During February 2011, our congregation was going through *40 Days Living the Jesus Creed,* a devotional style book by Scot McKnight that's designed to help individuals and groups truly absorb all that Jesus is trying to teach with the Jesus Creed. Each week we heard transformational stories of people applying the Jesus Creed by putting God first and loving their neighbors as themselves.

I'm still not sure how we were able to do it, but somehow we convinced Scot to leave snowy Chicago to come speak to our congregation about his book and hear about the impact it was having on our church family. During his message that Sunday, Scot examined the story in Mark chapter 12 where a scribe *(think lawyer)* asked Jesus a question: "Of all the commandments, which is the greatest or the most important one of all?" Jesus quickly replied quoting Deuteronomy 6:4-5—the *Shema* or the first half of the Jesus Creed. This probably didn't take the scribe by surprise. Any devout Jew of the day would recite these verses several times a day. It would be the first thing on their lips in the morning, and the last thing they would say at night, as well as several other times during the day.

But Jesus continued by quoting Leviticus 19:18, "You shall love your neighbor as yourself..." *(Maybe someday Christians will be known within the GLBT community for quoting this verse instead of Leviticus 20:13.)* As we walked through the text, I constructed a mental checklist:

- Do I believe there is only one God? *Yes I do.*
- Do I love God with all of my heart? *Yes I do.*
- Do I love God with all of my soul? *Yes I do.*
- Do I love God with all of my mind? *Yes I do.*
- Do I love God with all of my strength or (more literally) with every part of my being? *No, I do not.*

I had to be honest. I don't love God with *everything* right now. I'm drawn to 1 John 4:18 that says:

"There is no fear in love;

but perfect love casts out fear,

because fear involves torment.

But he who fears has not been made

perfect in love."

I know I can never attain perfect love. But right now I'm significantly lacking in love because I'm holding on to fear—and it's tormenting me. I don't trust God with my son. Holding on to the fear and not trusting God is like holding on to the blade of a knife. The tighter my grip, the worse the unintended consequences become.

"For I know the thoughts that I think toward you,

says the LORD,

thoughts of peace and not of evil, to give you

a future and a hope."

(Jeremiah 29:11)

As I look down the path of my son's life, I don't see "peace" nor a "future," and certainly not "hope." I see rejection by gays for being Christian and rejection by Christians for being gay. I see him being tormented in the crossfire of not only a national but an international issue that will only lead to strife and conflict. If my son were born in Uganda, I would fear for his life. Instead, I fear for his heart turning bitter toward a God who appears to have cast him adrift. As I began to head down the path of despair, I acknowledged that I've made my son's sexuality "the" issue. Yet God was now telling me that the REAL issue is "Do you love Me with every ounce of your being?"

Phileo to *Agape*

Setting the Scene for John 21: Jesus was beaten and brutally murdered on a cross, while the disciples (including Peter) scattered with all of their hopes dashed. Things had not turned out as they expected. On the third day, Jesus rose from the dead and showed himself to the disciples. Eight days later (John 20:26), Jesus appeared to the disciples again and "doubting Thomas" had his faith restored.

Now chapter 21 starts off with "After these things…," which seems to indicate that some time had passed. Peter, not knowing what to do, decided to go back to what was familiar to him: fishing. Some of the other disciples went with him, and they spent the entire night fishing but catching nothing. In the early hours of the morning, Jesus met up with them, and they shared breakfast over an open fire along the shore. It's during this quiet moment that Jesus engages Peter—who's exhausted after fishing all night and now has a stomach full of breakfast—in the following conversation found in John 21:15-17.

Jesus asked, "Peter, do you love Me?" It loses a little in the English translation, as we have only one word for *love*. But Jesus was asking Peter if he loved Him with a love *(agapao)* that is reserved only for God.

Peter responded, "Yes, Lord, I love You." But Peter used a different word for *love (phileo)*, which is more aligned with a brotherly love. (This is where we get the name *Philadelphia*, the City of Brotherly Love. Having grown up in the suburbs of the city that once booed and threw snowballs at Santa Claus during an Eagles game, I see the irony of this.)

Jesus asked Peter a second time, "Peter, do you *agapao* Me?"

"Yes, Lord, I *phileo* You."

In order to get Peter's attention, Jesus asked a third time and changed the wording: "Peter, do you *Philadelphia* Me?"

By now Peter is grieved because the third time Jesus asked him, He used *phileo* instead of *agapao*. "Jesus, You know everything, You know that I *phileo* You." Knowing that the correct answer comes with using *agapao*, Peter still cannot bring himself to say the Jesus Creed to its fullest— that he love God with his "everything." Although Peter is remembered as the disciple exhibiting the most faith, he also stumbled pretty badly—and his denial of Jesus (three times) on the night before He was crucified may have still been on Peter's heart and mind. Yes, even Peter knew that he came up short. But Jesus didn't chastise him. Jesus didn't continue to press Peter for the *right* response. Jesus simply said, "Feed My sheep." *Peter, will you take care of those who belong to Me? Peter, will you* agapao *your neighbor?*

It's Time for a SHIFT

I need to move away from my own anxieties and fears to trusting God.

> "Be anxious for nothing,
> but in everything by prayer and supplication,
> with thanksgiving,
> let your requests be made known to God."
> (Philippians 4:6)

On the prayer continuum of Surrender—Intercession—Control, my prayer life needs to SHIFT from my current position (somewhere between intercession and trying to control God). I call these "hedge of protection prayers." Instead, my prayers need to be positioned somewhere between surrender and intercession, what I call "let His light shine prayers."

I also need to SHIFT my son's sexuality from being "the" issue to being "an" issue. While I'm not trying to minimize or ignore its impact on our lives, I have to recognize that there are significantly more verses in the Bible that talk about pride or greed than talk about sexuality.

I need to SHIFT from *phileo*-ing God to *agapao*-ing God. The Jesus Creed resolves in a perfect cadence when I SHIFT to loving God with "my everything." Your words *are* true. You do think thoughts of peace and not evil, and so I resolve to accept that You are in control. I will *agapao* God, even if I don't get my way, even if this doesn't go the way I think it should. I will *agapao* with all my strength. As Abraham did with his son Isaac, I give You my son—*unconditionally*.

I drop to my knees in my own puddle of tears,
and beckon You on behalf of my son.
I surrender

Sleep taunts me, my stomach is a cauldron of grief,

I beseech You save my son from this pain.

I surrender

Long ago, I surrendered my own life

and You brightened my soul.

On this journey, I've surrendered many things

to You,

but I have hidden the most precious;

Hoping to satisfy You with lesser sacrifices.

Oh, Lord, I will surrender anything else,

even my own life.

My thoughts scream.

Slowly You unfurl my fist,

carefully prying open my clenched fingers,

one-by-one.

Wincing I feel the anguish

from holding that position for so long.

And when my palm is at last extended,

I find my son inside.

Yet, You do not take him.

You require that I make the transfer myself.

Your hand rests next to mine, patiently waiting.

Bigger, stronger, infinitely more steady.

The creases in Your palm,

the very mountains and caverns of the earth itself.

It is time.

Glancing around,

I search for something else to place in Your palm.

I see none.

But through this trial I have learned

I can never provide what my son truly needs.

And because of this pain,

I have the strength to make the transfer.

As I place him in Your hand,

You whisper a reminder of a substitute already

made

A similar grief endured.

A solitary, universal sacrifice.

For me…for my son

…*for everyone in the GLBT community.*

Surrender brings peace.

My son rests in Your sovereign, everlasting hands.

And now I will rest and bless Your name forever.

—Author Unknown

Ministry to Vocation

Quoting Os Guinness, Scot McKnight writes in *The Jesus Creed*:

"The truth is not that God is finding us a place for our gifts but that God has created us and our gifts for a place of His choosing—and we will only be ourselves when we are finally there."[103]

While I've enjoyed doing children's *ministry*, I've come to realize that God has equipped me and called me to a *vocation* of shepherding. "Feed My sheep." While this may not have been the most important, it was the first SHIFT I recognized that needed to be addressed. It was also the most visible and had implications with regard to how I do my job. Mother Teresa spent years moving from ministry (teacher of young girls) to vocation (The Saint of the Gutters). It's what she labeled as her "call within a call." I'm fortunate to work with a great team of leaders who also recognize the need for this shift and are willing to shift their own ministries to make it happen. Still, it will take some time to complete it, and the process is complicated by its impact on multiple staff members. While my desire may be for quick relief, my heart is to make the SHIFT that will gain lasting spiritual formation.

Seeker Sensitive to Seeker Intentional

For the Birds is Pixar's animated short film about a group of small birds congregating on a cable suspended between two electrical poles. As each bird exhibits its own personality, we see how the birds are different, yet very much the same. Along comes a rather large bird who's awkward but friendly, and he'd like to join the conversation up on that wire. Chirping amongst each other, the smaller birds begin discussing the matter, as if to say, "Look at him! He's obviously one of us (a bird), yet he's *very* different."

Undeterred, the larger bird tries to win their friendship by flying up and landing right in the middle of the group. But his weight pulls the cable down almost to the ground, causing all of the smaller birds to slide uncomfortably close to each other—and the odd stranger. So the birds begin chirping in frustration and decide to push this familiar stranger out, causing him to eventually hang upside down by his feet. So the two nearest birds begin pecking his toes to try to make him let go of the wire. Meanwhile, the other birds egg these two on and chant their support in unison. One by one the birds begin to notice the extent to which the wire is stretched, and then it slowly dawns on them what will happen when that last toe lets go of the wire.

The large bird gives one last good-natured honk to his friends before finally letting go. And when the larger bird gently drops the short distance to the ground, the little birds are catapulted into the sky. A mass of feathers drifts to the ground as the audience anticipates the return of a flock of naked birds. The first bird lands and is obviously embarrassed by his featherless state. So the larger bird helpfully hands him a leaf to cover up. As naked birds now rain down from the sky, each one races to hide behind the big bird who's now chuckling at his new friends.

Scot McNight, in his book *The Blue Parakeet*, calls these awkward birds *familiar strangers*.[104] They walk among us and even seem familiar somehow, yet they are strangers. Thus, we aren't really sure how to interact with them. Scot goes on to make the comparison of how we Christians feel uncomfortable fellowshipping with people who are a little different than we are. Christians disagree on a variety of issues, such as women in ministry, baptism by immersion versus sprinkling, pre-Trib or post-Trib, the use of one Bible translation as the only *inspired* acceptable version, and even the use of (God forbid) drums in church. We're uncomfortable in areas of disagreement, so we hop from church to church in search of the *perfect* home where we might agree on every issue. Disappointment follows.

Some of these familiar strangers are different because they hold a view that's contrary to ours on a particular theological or ethical issue. Other birds in our congregation are different only because we don't know what to do with them. There is the single mom who struggles to get her tribe to church on Sundays. There is the man who's celebrating one month of sobriety and whose world is starting to come into focus. He's experienced firsthand the unmerited favor of God. These are people whose life circumstances have put them in an awkward position of doing the best they can, yet falling short of the unwritten expectation of doing "church." Yet they're at church every Sunday, and most of the crowd greets them with a familiar smile as they walk strangely past them. They are welcome in our church, we are sensitive to the fact that they are seeking God, yet we are unaware of their fragile circumstances. We aren't actively engaged in helping them get any closer to this God we claim to serve.

My SHIFT is to move from being a seeker-sensitive *(unsensitive, if I'm honest with myself)* to a seeker-intentional person. I'm shifting from just being comfortable with the Blue Parakeets at our church to intentionally seeking them out.

In *Generous Justice*, Timothy Kelly writes:

> I would like to believe that a heart for the [*familiar stranger*] sleeps down in a Christian's soul until it is awakened. I think the reason that this sensibility has not been more aroused in the Christian world is due to the failure of my own class, pastors and Christian leaders. I believe when justice for the [*familiar stranger*] is connected not to guilt but to grace and to the gospel, this "pushes the button" down deep in believers' souls and they begin to wake up.[105]

This has become a Defining Moment, a spiritual marker for me. This is my personal nonnegotiable: I want to become a pastor to the pastor-less and a shepherd to the shepherd-less by reaching out to the Blue Parakeets who walk among us, as well as the *wild* parakeets who are my neighbors.

From Silence to Stillness

According to Dictionary.com, the most common definition of *silence* is "absence of any sound or noise; stillness." But what I've been feeling is closer to the latter definition, "the state of being forgotten; oblivion: *in the news again after years of silence.*" But *stillness* is "the absence of motion" or "windlessness." In Hebrews 13:5 God affirms: *"I will never leave you nor forsake you."* My perception of the desert has now shifted from that of a barren wasteland that should be exited as soon as possible, to a fertile training ground blossoming with opportunities for me to experience God in a manner that has been atypical for me in the past. I shift from a sense of God's "abandonment" to that of God's stillness, causing me to strain my senses in a desperate search for God.

But listen carefully to the sound of your loneliness
Like a heartbeat drives you mad
In the stillness of remembering
What you had

And what you lost.

—Fleetwood Mac, "Dreams"[106]

In the sounds of my loneliness, it is my own heartbeat that drives me insane only reaffirming my sense of *abandonment*. But it is in the stillness that I remember what I had, a close interaction with the Creator of the universe. That which was lost *must* be found at *all* costs making this "the" issue. I will be patient in the stillness. God's presence in the stillness remains palatable, if not tangible.

Typical to Atypical

With regard to the issue of sexuality, Christians and churches have been labeled as "typical," meaning "judgmental." By default, Christians continue to wear the judgmental label by their lack of engagement in this issue. Passive rejection of this label is not an option. It requires an intentional SHIFT away from the typical.

> I've lived through my share of misfortune
> And I've worked in the blazing sun
> But how long should it take somebody
> Before they can be someone

'Cause I know there's got to be another level

Somewhere closer to the other side

And I'm feeling like it's now or never

Can I break the spell of the *typical, the typical, the*

typical

I'm the *typical*

I'm the *typical*

—Mutemath, "Typical"[107]

Churches *typically* don't send missionaries into the jungles of Papua New Guinea to picket and protest the tribal practice of child sacrifice. Common sense dictates that this method would not be effective. So where is the rationale that this [picketing] is effective with other people groups?

Recently in the news, there was some controversy over the porn industry's expo in Las Vegas. What made the *typical* headline news was the group of church people picketing outside the event. What didn't make the evening news was the *atypical* church group that rented a booth in the expo. Here passersby were greeted with a bottle of water and encouraged to stop in if they needed or wanted anyone to pray for them. Period! Love *shifts* from judgment to grace. Grace is not conditional. Grace is not white or black. Grace is not male or female. Grace is not heterosexual or homosexual. Grace is available to all who desire it.

> "Let us therefore come boldly to the throne
> of grace,
> that we may obtain mercy
> and find grace to help in time of need."
> (Hebrews 4:16)

> "With heads held high,
> let us enter the eternal storehouse of grace and fill
> our bins to overflowing with grace and mercy,
> which we so desperately need now!"
> (The Chris Rader translation of Hebrews 4:16)

I am filling my bins with grace and preparing for a long season of vocation.

Reputation to Identity

When talking about one's reputation, today's social media is nothing compared to the impact of gossip in the ancient world. Joseph's impeccable reputation had earned him the title *tsadiq*, which in Hebrew is translated as "a righteous man." Although he and Mary had not yet come together, their tradition considered them legally married. While getting pregnant before marriage doesn't raise too many eyebrows in today's society, back then it was a deal-killer that could ruin the reputation of a *tsadiq*. By law, Mary and her seducer should be taken out behind the woodshed and stoned to death. But Joseph chose to disobey the law *and* his interpretation of it, which was pretty clear, and put her away privately instead. That is, get a divorce.

> "Then Joseph her husband,
> being a just *man* [*tsadiq*]
> and not wanting to make her a public example,
> was minded to put her away secretly."
> (Matthew 1:19)

Mercy trumped justice. *Afterward* an angel appeared to Joseph and told him not to fear, that what Mary had said regarding the baby being conceived by the Holy Spirit was true. While Mary and Joseph had privileged information that transcended current truth (the law), it's doubtful that their Facebook community would restore either of their reputations based on their "truth."

"Sometimes the implication of listening to the

voice of God

is that we ruin our reputation in the public square."

—Scot McKnight, *The Jesus Creed*[108]

My identification (in Christ) trumps my reputation (before people). Time for a SHIFT.

Resolve to Un-resolve

This is not as much about living life with unresolved issues as it is about taking a "resolved" issue back off the shelf for re-examination. It doesn't mean I'll change my conclusions. It doesn't mean my previous level of evaluation was insufficient. But it *does* mean I'm open to the possibility that I may have brought this issue to a premature resolve based on misinformation or incomplete information. While I believe in the inerrant Word of God, I do not believe in my inerrant *interpretation* of God's Word. My core values and beliefs have not changed, but my sense of certainty about those beliefs may come into question.

"This means that we can expect that our

sense of certainty

about our beliefs will ebb and flow.

Sometimes doubt will come."

—John Ortberg, *Faith and Doubt*[109]

I have to be willing to live in the tension of uncertainty. But I find it confusing to observe very prominent theologians, scholars, pastors, and teachers I respect landing on the opposite side of an issue. How can these brilliant men and women look at the same passage of Scripture and come to such different conclusions? Each of them bases their conclusions on their interpretation and evaluation of Scripture. Regardless of the issue, some very smart people have resolved difficult ethical issues by coming to very different conclusions. I've talked with gay men who are supportive of same-sex marriages. I've also talked with gay men who, after examining the Scriptures, have concluded that same-sex marriage is not God's plan for them. And you don't have to go too far to find a straight man who isn't okay with same-sex marriages regardless of his religious beliefs.

But the most confusing of all is a heterosexual man who, after examining the Scriptures, believes that same-sex marriage is acceptable by God. Here is a person who has nothing to gain by his position and everything to lose (assuming he's a member of a conservative church…*soon to be ex-member!*).

So I find myself in the open cadence between theology and sexuality. I know my son's heart. I know his reputation as a godly young man. I see his faith. I hear a heart that wants to follow God. I see a young man wrestling with God and not letting go until he receives a blessing. I see a bulldog tenacity of not letting go of God even when his reality and theology collide and it would be easier to just let go. I pull my theology of sexuality back off the shelf and place it in a state of un-resolve. As I go back to Scripture and look for *anything* dealing with sexuality, I can't help but stumble over so many verses on grace.

When I shifted from "believer" to "follower" almost 25 years ago, my foul language didn't stop overnight. My sexual promiscuity didn't change overnight, either. What would be the result if we took a poll of an average Sunday congregation with just one question:

Have you had sexual relations outside of marriage
since you became a Christ-follower?

My guess would be that a large portion of the congregation would answer "Yes". And many, if they answered truthfully, would have to say they're *still* involved in sexual relations outside of marriage despite *knowing* that the Bible *and* their interpretation of the Bible are very clear on that issue. So why is there grace for the heterosexual who gets his girlfriend pregnant but not for the homosexual? I need to SHIFT from judgment to grace and from resolved to un-resolved.

The First Cry

A little boy is jolted awake at the sound of words being hurled back and forth. It's late and Dad has just returned home to an expected but undesired conversation. While the words aren't discernable through the thin wall separating the boy's room from his parents', there is a cadence to the conversation that says *We have been here before*.

Tonight is different. The volume is higher. The tension has climaxed. Adrenaline has removed any vestige of this young boy's sleepiness. With his heart beating faster, his breaths getting shorter, and his ears at the ready, Mom's words are unmistakable*: "Say good-bye to the kids before you leave."*

A few heavy footsteps, a firm hand on the doorknob, and then a stream of light dispels a room full of darkness as the door creaks open. All the air in his little room is vanquished as Dad takes a deep breath and prepares his words. But words become unnecessary as their eyes lock. The furrowed brow on this young father of four communicates everything.

Fear turns to panic as the boy's body begins to heave and convulse in tears of pain. The chords of dissonance crash like cymbals in his head.

A thousand tears fall before two strong arms reach down and enfold the young boy into the broad chest of his father. Words are whispered into his ear.

His fragile frame is carried into his parents' room and gently laid on the bed. Lying on the far side, Mom begins to tuck him in. Then Dad slips under the covers and spreads his massive wing over the nest ensuring their safety.

Moments of rest are repeatedly interrupted for fear
of what might happen should sleep overcome.

Whispers are exchanged.

There is a cadence that indicates an authentic resolve. Tears subside. Sleep is victorious over fear.

Fear shifts to trust.

Tenuous Fatherhood shifts to *Unconditional Dad*.

This is a Defining Moment.

Thus ends the first cry.

Selah

*S*elah is a Hebrew term that means "to give pause." It's mostly used in the book of Psalms to indicate to the reader that this is a good place to pause and let what you've just read sink in. There might also be value in going back to reread, rethink, and perhaps apply what you've just read to your own life before marching ahead to finish the chapter.

In the musical sense, it's the pause, the space between "shave and a haircut" and "two bits." It's the notes *not* played—although anticipated—that carry the most significance. If the pause is too short, the dramatic effect is missed. If the pause is too long, the moment is lost.

As I pause and reflect on the previous chapters, the following are some thoughts that come to mind.

Defining Moments aren't meant to crush us, but rather to alter our course of direction. Meteors have a way of reducing *our* plan for life to rubble. It's up to us to decide if those meteors will demolish us or if we'll live through them and adjust our lives to God's plan. *I wonder what that football star was meant to live through?* Having a bigger God-perspective on our circumstances is important, yet not always enough. Job's wife had a God-perspective (as opposed to luck-perspective), yet her view of God was limited. She believed God is there only to answer her prayers and protect her from *bad luck*. So when faced with a Defining Moment, what she does next reveals her core beliefs of God: *"Curse God and die."* Her view of God was no better than someone else's belief in luck. I'm making a conscious decision to put my faith in action and trust that there is more going on with this situation than God has revealed. I need to let God be God and follow Him, rather than trying to lead. What I was meant to live through will be revealed in His timing. *Selah.*

Our actions come out of our core values. As with the football star, what makes some people take the ultimate out (suicide)? What is at the heart or the very core of a person that makes him or her respond one way versus another? To let go or grab on? The only way to know the core of one's beliefs is to watch that person make choices under pressure.[110] That is where faith turns into action. Action means... making adjustments in my life to accommodate the impact of a meteor. That means I make a decision to move in a certain direction based on a belief that there is a God, that there is a purpose to my situation even if I don't see it. The impact of being hit by a meteor ultimately has a positive *eternal* impact and will work out for good.[111] As with Job's situation, we aren't always aware of the spiritual dimensions to our circumstances. But my decisions and actions must be made in the direction of faith and based on the foundational value that there is a God who does care. My faith allows me to step out in boldness and courage when my intellectual reasoning has run dry. *Selah.*

I am encouraged to be strong in grace, not judgment. Why is this atypical in the church? If the church is saved by grace, then why does it not live by grace?[112] I am sensing a great deal of responsibility to not get this one wrong and the increasing probability of not getting it right. My Golden Retriever (faithful companion) personality recognizes that no matter which direction I choose and no matter how my church decides to respond, there are certain people groups (inside the church and outside) that will be offended. I'm not interested in trying to please people (although I'd sleep better at night if I could). Rather, I'm compelled not only to represent Christ to those who show up on Sunday mornings, but also be intentional about showing grace to my neighbor. I don't question the authority of Scripture; however, I do question my ability to interpret and rightly discern *all* of Scripture. And regardless of my interpretation, I still have the issue of "Where do I go from here?" How do I represent Christ to families who've been impacted by the meteor of homosexuality? How do I communicate unconditional love for my son? This is no longer a theological debate for me. It's time to put my faith in action. Ignoring the issue is not an option. *Selah*.

Two Bits

Heal my heart and make it clean

Open up my eyes to the things unseen

Show me how to love like You have loved me

Break my heart for what breaks Yours

Everything I am for Your kingdom's cause

As I walk from earth into eternity

Hosanna, hosanna

Hosanna in the highest[113]

In Mark 14, beginning in verse 32, Jesus takes his followers with Him into the garden named Gethsemane. He wants them to spend some time in prayer over the coming events leading to the cross. He calls Peter, James, and John out of the group of guys and asks them to walk a little bit further with Him. Jesus becomes "exceedingly sorrowful, *even to death*" (v. 34). Asking them to watch and pray, Jesus separates Himself a little, falls on the ground, and begins to pray:

"Abba, Father, all things are possible for You.

Take this cup away from Me;

nevertheless, not what I will but what You will."

(Mark 14:36)

Jesus understands what's at stake, the eternal implications for creation, and the work that will be done on the cross. But there is also an awareness of the harsh reality of having to go down that path. "Father...isn't there any other way?" There has to be another way to accomplish the same task, one that is significantly less painful. Isn't there an easier way? There is an eternal open cadence, this unresolved separation between Creator and creation that has both sides yearning for the progression from dissonance to consonance. The cross beckons for a perfect resolve. Any other way would be a deceptive cadence leaving this issue open-ended.

It was the ninth hour and darkness had fallen over the land. Jesus' body had been badly beaten and was nailed to a cross for all to see. He cried out:

> "'Eloi, Eloi, lama sabachthani?'
> which is translated,
> *'My God, My God, why have You forsaken me?'*"
> (Mark 15:34)

Jesus had a moment of *interior darkness*, God's silence. God's stillness. A sense of abandonment, yet the master plan (the Master's plan) is about to be fulfilled.

After Jesus' death and resurrection, He appeared to His followers and told them to:

> "Go into all the world and preach the gospel to
> every creature.
> He who believes and is baptized will be saved;
> but he who does not believe will be condemned."
> (Mark 16:15-16)

This is what's known in Christian circles as the "Great Commission." The "Great Commandment" is *to love God*

with your everything and to love your neighbor as yourself.
The Great Commission is then to *go tell other people the*
Good News! God has removed all of the tension between
Creator and creation. History has been resolved. The cadence
has been made perfect. God has added His *two bits.* We can
expect no more. As the final scenes of life are completed,
there aren't any new subplots being developed. There aren't
any new characters being introduced. The storyline of each
person on the stage of life is playing out to a final resolve
with their Creator.

My charter as a Christ-Follower is to love God and love
my neighbor. How do I love my neighbor? By telling people
wherever I go that His-story ends well. Some will believe the
story and be drawn in. Others will not. There is an element
of free choice that is difficult to comprehend. Why would
people *not* want to be restored to their Creator? How did
the message become so complicated? Why do we put unnecessary prerequisites in front of people that we ourselves
weren't willing (or able) to do? Where did the Good News
of God's grace get turned into judgment and condemnation?

As I contemplate what's in store for myself in this next
year, I find myself saying: "Lord, is there any other way?"
I guess I could ignore this sexuality issue and go back to

my "ministry." I could pull a Jonah and just take a cruise to Hawaii to live out the "good life." Not only would this be thumbing my nose at God, but Jonah's voyage didn't turn out so well, as I recall, and God's purpose for Jonah was fulfilled in spite of his stubbornness. Ignoring God's call or willfully going in the opposite direction will not exempt me from the two-fold pain that's gnawing away at my soul. The first source of pain is the fact that this issue has hit home. To ignore it is to ignore my son. Not an option! The second source of pain is that God has broken my heart for what breaks His: A group of people who would *believe* if it weren't for all of the *typical* Christians getting in the way.

So how do I navigate this issue in the coming year? As soon as I finish writing this book, what do I do? I could abandon my current beliefs and just accept same-sex attraction as being God-ordained and part of God's "A" Plan. While that might give me favor with some folks, it will certainly cause division with others. It may give me cause to demonize *typical* Christians who'd suggest that I stone my son and all of *those people* to death. That doesn't seem to bring anything into harmony. In fact, it seems to foster more of the current tension that I desire to resolve.

I suppose I could retreat deeper into the mind-set of "God said it, I believe it, that settles it." That might provide a temporary (albeit false) sense of peace within Christian circles. I'm sure I could play the self-righteous card and cast out all of those "sinners"—even at the expense of my own son. But following that train to its final destination would require that I disassociate with everyone who disagrees with me on *every* theological and ethical issue. That would make me a very lonely man in the Church of One.

It appears that the only real option is to have radical honesty and acceptance. My approval or disapproval of same-sex relations, while it may leave an open cadence with which to do life with my neighbor, ultimately has no bearing on eternity. While this past year has stirred up my theological pot of beliefs, so far none of those core beliefs have changed significantly. But the manner in which I *live out* the Great Commandment and the Great Commission has made a radical shift.

Most people want what I want: A place to connect spiritually. A place or a group of people who will accept me as I am with all of my brokenness and regardless of my sexuality, regardless of my "whatever." Living out the *Jesus Creed* or making decisions about faith is not about winning debates.

According to John Ortberg, it's more like making a wager at the roulette table. We all have something riding on the outcome.[114]

There are two reasons this book was self-published. For one, I've never authored a book before and no publisher would consider taking a chance on me. *It's hard to get past that one!* Second, the evidence of a wounded soul is intentionally left exposed. Jagged edges remain unpolished. I'm not writing this to become a famous author. In fact, it's personally cost me several thousand dollars to print what's in your hands right now, with little expectation of recouping my cost.

Having turned the big "50" in the midst of writing this book, I began looking at people who became known for their accomplishments *after* the age of 50. Ronald Reagan and Laura Ingalls Wilder are just a couple of the people who also accomplished things before age 50, much of which we are either unaware of or are only vaguely familiar with today. They're definitely better known for what they did after 50.

Perhaps when I die and the scrolls of life are opened, the matter of sexuality and Christianity will be *my* issue. Yet if I could choose *my* issue, it would not be this one. I would choose to be a famous Hollywood star. That's pretty ironic when you consider the fact that Ronald Reagan was an actor before age 50, but he likely won't be remembered for his movie career. Perhaps that's why God had to break my heart for what breaks His.

So this year you might see me at San Diego's Gay Pride Parade. No, I won't be holding a sign that says REPENT! And I won't be pole-dancing naked on a float either. I will, however, be down where the parade starts handing out water bottles with a smile. I'll also be waiting, praying, and making myself available should someone have a Defining Moment. And that's my two bits!

Acknowledgments

L aura: For your unconditional love and support, which is measured in the difficult seasons of life. Your smile still captivates me. Thank you for providing hope beyond the depression and the encouragement to keep moving forward.

Dean: For your all-out prayers for my son, your insights, and your friendship. Thanks for helping me find laughter again. For all of those trips back and forth to Home Depot to get that "one last item" we didn't think of, and for all the great conversations over a burrito. I pray the fence will serve you and Sam for a long time.

Archie: For being a shoulder to lean on and for your friendship and laughter. Thank you for stretching the boundaries of unconditional love for your son and being an example of an atypical Christian man.

Tedd: For your faithfulness in allowing God to use you to provide a Safe Passage for people and families navigating the Journey of sexuality and the Bible. Thank you for your mentoring as I prepare to start a similar Safe Place at our church.

My Accountability Group: Mark: For more than 12 years of accountability and friendship as we hike Cowles Mountain every Saturday morning. Thanks for dragging me up the hill and helping me keep things in perspective. For Steve, Kenneth and Jim: Thanks for the many miles of friendship.

Greg: For your friendship through the years. Thanks for letting me "slime" you at camp.

Jim L.: For your faithful friendship and support for our family. And thanks for letting us crash at your home every New Year's to watch the Rose Parade.

Jim H.: For Padres games and "therapy" sessions at Hodad's and various other restaurants across town. Thanks for your consistent friendship through the years.

Ed: For your wisdom, understanding, and—above all—your willingness to do ministry in the open cadences of life.

Laura G., Dave U., and Janet: For helping me turn a journal into a book.

Sherman (my dog): For your companionship during all of those early morning writing sessions.

Seth and Steven: My sons. I love you both. Unconditionally.

Bibliography

Albom, Mitch. *Have a Little Faith: A True Story*. New York: Hyperion, 2009.

Anderson, Kerby. *A Biblical Point of View on Homosexuality*. Eugene, OR: Harvest House, 2008.

Bernstein, Robert A. *Straight Parents, Gay Children: Keeping Families Together*. New York: Thunder's Mouth Press, 2003.

Blackaby, Henry T., and Claude V. King. *Experiencing God: Knowing and Doing the Will of God*. Nashville, TN: LifeWay Press, 1990.

Bogle, Darlene. *Strangers in a Christian Land*. Old Tappan, NJ: Chosen Books, 1990.

Bottke, Allison. *Setting Boundaries with Your Adult Children: Six Steps to Hope and Healing for Struggling Parents.* Eugene, OR: Harvest House, 2008.

Chambers, Alan. *God's Grace and the Homosexual Next Door: Reaching the Heart of the Gay Men and Women in Your World.* Eugene, OR: Harvest House, 2006.

Cloud, Henry and John Townsend. *Boundaries.* Grand Rapids, MI: Zondervan, 1995.

Dallas, Joe. *Desires in Conflict: Hope for Men Who Struggle with Sexual Identity.* Eugene, OR: Harvest House, 2003.

George, Bill with Peter Sims. *True North: Discover Your Authentic Leadership.* San Francisco, Jossey-Bass, 2007.

Hybels, Bill. *The Power of a Whisper: Hearing God, Having the Guts to Respond.* Grand Rapids, MI: Zondervan, 2010.

Johnson, Barbara. *I'm So Glad You Told Me What I Didn't Wanna Hear.* Dallas: Word, 1996.

Keller, Timothy. *Generous Justice: How God's Grace Makes Us Just.* New York: Dutton, 2010.

Konrad, Jeff. *You Don't Have to Be Gay.* Hilo, HI: Pacific Publishing House, 1992.

Manion, Jeff. *The Land Between: Finding God in Difficult Transitions.* Grand Rapids, MI: Zondervan, 2010.

Marin, Andrew. *Love Is an Orientation: Elevating the Conversation with the Gay Community.* Downers Grove, IL: IVP Books, 2009.

McKnight, Scot. *The Blue Parakeet: Rethinking How You Read the Bible.* Grand Rapids, MI: Zondervan, 2008.

McKnight, Scot. *The Jesus Creed: Loving God, Loving Others.* Brewster, MA: Paraclete, 2004.

Miller, Donald. *A Million Miles in a Thousand Years: How I Learned to Live a Better Story.* Nashville, TN: Thomas Nelson, 2009.

Mother Teresa. *Mother Teresa: Come Be My Light.* Edited by Brian Kolodiejchuk, M. C. New York: DoubleDay, 2007.

Ortberg, John. *Faith and Doubt.* Grand Rapids, MI: Zondervan, 2008.

Ortberg, John. *The Me I Want to Be: Becoming God's Best Version of You.* Grand Rapids, MI: Zondervan, 2009.

Ortberg, John. *When the Game Is Over, It All Goes Back in the Box.* Grand Rapids, MI: Zondervan, 2007.

Seamands, David A. *Living With Your Dreams: Let God Restore Your Shattered Dreams*. Wheaton, IL: Victor Books, 1990.

Sherrill, John and Elizabeth. *The Hiding Place: The Triumphant True Story of Corrie Ten Boom*. New York: Bantam, 1974.

Thompson, Chad W. *Loving Homosexuals as Jesus Would: A Fresh Christian Approach*. Grand Rapids, MI: Brazos, 2004.

Tyler, Cheryl Moss. *And You Invited Me In*. New York: Atria Books, 2008.

Warren, Rick. *The Purpose Driven Life*. Grand Rapids, MI: Zondervan, 2002.

White, James R. and Jeffrey D. Niell. *The Same Sex Controversy: Defending and Clarifying the Bible's Message About Homosexuality*. Minneapolis: Bethany House, 2002.

Endnotes

1. Yancey, *Reaching for the Invisible God*, 96.

2. *Sua Sponte* is Latin for "of their own accord." Predominantly used as a legal term, it's also the regimental motto for the 75th Ranger Regiment of the U.S. Army Rangers. It refers to the Rangers' choice to accept their fate and move ahead with little to no prompting. I chose this.

3. Men…De is a construct of the Greek language which has the effect of saying, "On the one hand, *this*. On the other hand, *that*." This is illustrated in Acts 12:5—*(On the one hand)*, Peter was kept in prison. *(On the other hand)*, the church was earnestly praying to God for him.

4. Jeremiah 1:5 says, "Before I formed you in the womb I knew you."

5. Romans 3:10 "As it is written: *There is none righteous, no, not one*." Romans 3:23 "For all have sinned and fall short of the glory of God."

6. John 3:16 "For God so loved the world that He gave His only begotten Son, that whoever believes in Him should not perish but have everlasting life."

7. John 5:24 "Most assuredly, I say to you, he who hears My word and believes in Him who sent Me has everlasting life, and shall not come into judgment, but has passed from death into life."

8. Ephesians 1:4 "Just as He chose us in Him before the foundation of the world, that we should be holy and without blame before Him in love."

9. No Bible reference; just a direct quote from my wife!

10. 2 Corinthians 3:18 "But we all, with unveiled face, beholding as in a mirror the glory of the Lord, are being transformed into the same image from glory to glory, just as by the Spirit of the Lord."

11. Hebrews 13:5 "For He Himself has said, *'I will never leave you nor forsake you.'*"

12. Isaiah 55:8-9 "'For My thoughts *are* not your thoughts, Nor *are* your ways My ways," says the LORD. 'For *as* the heavens are higher than the earth, so are My

ways higher than your ways, and My thoughts than your thoughts.'"

13. Romans 8:28 "And we know that all things work together for good to those who love God, to those who are the called according to *His* purpose."

14. Matthew 11:28 "Come to Me, all *you* who labor and are heavy laden, and I will give you rest."

15. Miller, *A Million Miles in a Thousand Years*, 70.

16. Proverbs 16:4 "The LORD has made all for Himself."

17. Job 2:10 "Shall we indeed accept good from God, and shall we not accept adversity?"

18. My paraphrase of Job 6:14 "To him who is afflicted, kindness *should be shown* by his friends."

19. "When you face a crisis of belief, what you do next reveals what you really believe about God." Blackaby and King, *Experiencing God*, 108.

20. Originally titled "Just a Weaver" by Benjamin Malacia Franklin (1882–1965), http://www.writersonthe-loose.com/writers/MK/index.cfm?story=32559.

21. John 14:6 "I am the way, the truth, and the life. No one comes to the Father except through Me."

22. Romans 10:9 "If you confess with your mouth the Lord Jesus and believe in your heart that God has raised Him from the dead, you will be saved."

23. Printed in Tim Hansel's *Holy Sweat* (Nashville, TN: W Publishing Group, 1987).

24. www.willowcreek.com (click on "Global Leadership Summit")

25. Romans 12:8 "He who leads, [do so] with diligence..."

26. Manion, *The Land Between*, 16.

27. Exodus 3:8 "So I have come down to deliver them out of the hand of the Egyptians, and to bring them up from the land to a good and large land, to a land flowing with milk and honey..."

28. Manion, *The Land Between*, 16.

29. Ibid., 45.

30. Ibid., 55.

31. Philippians 4:13 "I can do all things through Christ who strengthens me."

32. Albom, *Have a Little Faith*, 98–99.

33. Mother Teresa, *Mother Teresa: Come Be My Light*, 22.

34. I love those little chocolate-covered (wax) donuts! I keep telling myself they are vitamins so I won't get sick

if I drink the water or have some tacos, etc. So far, they've worked!

35. Albom, *Have a Little Faith*, 181.

36. George, *True North: Discover Your Authentic Leadership*.

37. Genesis 3:8 "And they heard the sound of the LORD God walking in the garden in the cool of the day…"

38. Isaiah 55:6 "Seek the LORD while He may be found, Call upon Him while He is near." Proverbs 7:15 "So I came out to meet you, Diligently to seek your face."

39. Mother Teresa, *Mother Teresa: Come Be My Light*, 22.

40. Seamands, *Living With Your Dreams*, 77.

41. Ibid., quoting A. W. Tozer in *The Root of the Righteous* (Chicago: Moody Press, 1955), 127.

42. Mother Teresa, *Mother Teresa: Come Be My Light*, 187.

43. Blackaby and King, *Experiencing God*, 94.

44. Yancey, *Reaching for the Invisible God*, 91.

45. Seamands, *Living With Your Dreams*, 80.

46. Romans 10:9 "If you confess with your mouth the Lord Jesus and believe in your heart that God has raised Him from the dead, you will be saved."

47. James 2:19 "You believe that God is one. You do well; the demons also believe, and shudder." (NASB)

48. Blackaby and King, *Experiencing God*, 101.

49. Hybels, *The Power of a Whisper*, 125.

50. Blackaby and King, *Experiencing God*, 103.

51. Matthew 3:16 "When He had been baptized, Jesus came up immediately from the water; and behold, the heavens were opened to Him, and He saw the Spirit of God descending like a dove and alighting upon Him."

52. Matthew 13:45-46 "Again, the kingdom of heaven is like a merchant seeking beautiful pearls, who, when he had found one pearl of great price, went and sold all that he had and bought it."

53. Philippians 4:7 "And the peace of God, which surpasses all understanding, will guard your hearts and minds through Christ Jesus."

54. Matthew 28:19-20 "Go therefore and make disciples of all the nations, baptizing them in the name of the Father and of the Son and of the Holy Spirit, teaching them to observe all things that I have commanded you; and lo, I am with you always, *even* to the end of the age."

55. Johnson, *I'm So Glad You Told Me What I Didn't Wanna Hear*, 13.

56. Blackaby and King, *Experiencing God*, 127.

57. Genesis 15:5 "Then [the LORD] brought [Abram] outside and said, "Look now toward heaven, and count the stars if you are able to number them." And He said to him, "So shall your descendants be."

58. Chip Brogden, *The Spiritual Desert: How God's Purposes Are Fulfilled in Your Wilderness Experiences* (Canandaigua, NY: The School of Christ, 2010), Sermon Series on CD.

59. 1 Corinthians 3:9 "For we are God's fellow workers..."; 2 Corinthians 6:1 "We then, *as* workers together *with Him...*"

60. John Trent, Rick Osborne, and Kurt Bruner, *Spiritual Growth of Children* (Wheaton, IL: Tyndale, 2000), 87. The four main personality types are Lion (leaders, Choleric), Otter (playful, Sanguine), Beaver (workers, Melancholy), and Golden Retriever (faithful, Phlegmatic).

61. I thought I'd read a book by this name years ago, and I wanted to give credit where credit is due. However, when I went to look for it, there were thousands of books with very similar titles.

62. McKnight, *The Blue Parakeet*, 13.

63. Ibid., 94.

64. Bogle, *Strangers in a Christian Land*, 106.

65. Genesis 32:24-31 Jacob wrestled all night with God and walked away with a limp.

66. Johnson, *I'm So Glad You Told Me What I Didn't Wanna Hear*, 6.

67. Albom, *Have a Little Faith*, 93.

68. www.drpaulcoleman.com

69. Self-medicating, as in drinking alcohol. Having been a pastor for 15 years, I'd chosen not to drink in order to avoid being a stumbling block to those in our church with alcohol issues. But I went from drinking no beer to having up to three beers a week. Nothing serious enough to write home about, but the *reason* why I started to drink really concerned me.

70. Joel 2:28-29 "And it shall come to pass afterward That I will pour out My Spirit on all flesh; Your sons and your daughters shall prophesy, Your old men shall dream dreams, Your young men shall see visions. And also on My menservants and on *My* maidservants I will pour out My spirit in those days."

71. Marin, *Love Is an Orientation*, 132.

72. Romans 5:6-8 "For when we were still without strength, in due time Christ died for the ungodly. For scarcely

for a righteous man will one die; yet perhaps for a good man someone would even dare to die. But God demonstrates His own love toward us, in that while we were still sinners, Christ died for us."

73. Romans 3:23 "All have sinned and fall short of the glory of God."

74. Romans 6:23 "For the wages of sin *is* death, but the gift of God *is* eternal life in Christ Jesus our Lord."

75. Marin, *Love Is an Orientation*, 161.

76. Chambers, *God's Grace and the Homosexual Next Door*, 209.

77. This is a reference to the 2007 film *The Diving Bell and the Butterfly*, a translation French journalist Jean-Dominique Bauby's memoir. He suffered a massive stroke which left him with a condition called locked-in syndrome (i.e., his brain was cognitively functional, but he could only blink one eyelid. As a result, he felt "locked-in" as if he were inside one of those metal diving apparatuses floating below the surface of the ocean, unable to move...and where no one can hear his screams for help.

78. Ortberg, *When the Game Is Over, It All Goes Back in the Box*.

79. John 8:12 "Then Jesus spoke to them again, saying, 'I am the light of the world. He who follows Me shall not walk in darkness, but have the light of life.'"

80. Mother Teresa, *Mother Teresa: Come Be My Light*, 208.

81. A reference to the Sunday night TV variety show from the 1960s, *The Ed Sullivan Show*. One act in particular showed a juggler who could spin plates on sticks. As he added new plates, he went back and gave existing plates additional spins to keep them going. Sooner or later, he had too many plates to keep spinning and eventually they came crashing down.

82. By "un-resolve" I mean to take an issue that I "thought" was resolved and reexamine it. I am open to new information. My conclusions may or may not change, but that's not the issue. The issue is that I'm willing to reexamine things, rather than just assume my original conclusion was accurate.

83. Q. Rahman and G. D. Wilson, "Sexual orientation and the 2nd to 4th finger length ratio: evidence for organising effects of sex hormones or developmental instability?" *Psychoneuroendocrinology* 28(3) (April 2003): 288–303.

84. Pages 289–292 of the above-mentioned article in *Psychoneuroendocrinology*.

85. 1 Corinthians 6:9-11 "Do you not know that the unrighteous will not inherit the kingdom of God? Do not be deceived. Neither fornicators, nor idolaters, nor adulterers, nor homosexuals, nor sodomites, nor thieves, nor covetous, nor drunkards, nor revilers, nor extortioners will inherit the kingdom of God. And such were some of you. But you were washed, but you were sanctified, but you were justified in the name of the Lord Jesus and by the Spirit of our God."

86. Marin, *Love Is an Orientation*, 99.

87. Chambers, *God's Grace and the Homosexual Next Door*, 126.

88. Marin, *Love Is an Orientation*, 100.

89. 1 Peter 1:16 "Because it is written, *'Be holy, for I am holy.'*"

90. Chambers, *God's Grace and the Homosexual Next Door*, 122.

91. Dan Gilgoff, "Chick-fil-A Controversy Shines Light on Restaurant's Christian DNA," CNN Belief Blog, February 4, 2011, http://religion.blogs.cnn.com/2011/02/04/chick-fil-a-controversy-shines-light-on-restaurants-christian-dna/.

92. Marin, *Love Is an Orientation*, 88.

93. Ibid., 42. While this statistic is presented in Andrew Marin's book, I'm unable to verify the accuracy or the source of the original study.

94. Anderson, *A Biblical Point of View on Homosexuality*, 82.

95. Ortberg, *Faith and Doubt*, 34.

96. John 8:1-11 The story of a woman caught in adultery.

97. Nick Wing, "Clint McCance, Arkansas School Board Member, Wants 'Fags' to Commit Suicide," *The Huffington Post* (Posted October 27, 2010), http://www.huffingtonpost.com/2010/10/27/clint-mccance-anti-gay-facebook_n_774656.html.

98. Walt Kelly, *Pogo: We Have Met the Enemy and He Is Us* (New York: Simon & Schuster, 1987).

99. Warren, *The Purpose Driven Life*, 53.

100. Matthew 5:27-28 "You have heard that it was said, you shall not commit adultery: but I say to you that every one that looks on a woman to lust after her has committed adultery with her already in his heart." ASV

101. Ed Noble, Sr. Pastor at Journey Community Church, Series Title: SHIFT, February 2011.

102. McKnight, *The Jesus Creed*.

103. Ibid., 84. (Quoting Os Guinness)

104. McKnight, *The Blue Parakeet*, 24.

105. Keller, *Generous Justice*, 107. For the word *poor*, I exchanged the broader term *familiar stranger* borrowed from Scot McKnight's *The Blue Parakeet*.

106. Fleetwood Mac, "Dreams," *Rumors*, 1977.

107. Mutemath, "Typical," *Mutemath*, 2006.

108. McKnight, *The Jesus Creed*, 79.

109. Ortberg, *Faith and Doubt*, 71.

110. Miller, *A Million Miles in a Thousand Years*, 74.

111. Romans 8:28 "And we know that all things work together for good to those who love God, to those who are the called according to *His* purpose."

112. Ortberg, *The Me I Want to Be*, 34. "God's plan is not just for us to be *saved* by grace—it is for us to *live* by grace."

113. Brooke Fraser, "Hosanna," Hillsong Publishing, 2006.

114. Ortberg, *Faith and Doubt*, 34.

CPSIA information can be obtained at www.ICGtesting.com
264473BV00002B/6/P